2025
WITCH'S
DIARY

A Rockpool book
PO Box 252
Summer Hill
NSW 2130
Australia

rockpoolpublishing.com
Follow us! f ⟳ rockpoolpublishing
Tag your images with #rockpoolpublishing

Northern hemisphere edition
ISBN: 9781922785855

Published in 2024 by Rockpool Publishing
Copyright text © Flavia Kate Peters and Barbara Meiklejohn-Free 2024
Images from Shutterstock

Designed by Sara Lindberg, Rockpool Publishing
Typeset by Christine Armstrong, Rockpool Publishing
Edited by Lisa Macken

Note: All moon phases in this diary are based on Universal Coordinated
Time (UTC) and are also checked against several sources including www.
calendar-12.com/moon_phases/2025. Eclipses are checked against www.
timeanddate.com/eclipse/2025. To find specific information for your
location, we suggest consulting www.timeanddate.com.

Printed and bound in China
10 9 8 7 6 5 4 3 2 1

RECLAIMING THE MAGICK OF THE OLD WAYS

2025 WITCH'S DIARY

NORTHERN HEMISPHERE

FLAVIA KATE PETERS * BARBARA MEIKLEJOHN-FREE

ROCKPOOL

PIONEERS OF THE CRAFT

The *2025 Witch's Diary* honours all those who have given their lives to the craft. They are the founders, wisdom keepers, elders and leaders who have gone before us, ensuring that we today hold the sacred knowledge of the ancients despite the gruesome punishments many faced and still face in mainstream society and particular cultures for their beliefs.

Let us remember those seen and unseen, known and unknown, and give our undying gratitude to all those who have shone the light of magick through the darkness.

We witches stand side by side, strong in our beliefs while the ancestors walk beside us, and we are proud to call ourselves witches of the craft.

So mote it be.

HAIL AND WELCOME!

The *2025 Witch's Diary*, a magickal tool from which you can draw wisdom from the witches of the old ways, is relevant to the modern witch today and enables you to thrive in balance and harmony and with a sprinkle of very real magick.

Witches are everywhere. A witch is someone just like you, who has always been drawn to nature, who naturally hears the whispers of the ancestors though the breeze and who welcomes the rains, glorifies in the heat of the sun and connects with the nourishment of the earth. A witch embraces each season, rejoicing at every new bud during the first stirrings of spring, the harvest abundance that summer supplies and the falling leaves of autumn, and revels in the deep, dark mystery that accompanies the winter months.

A witch's heart sings at the mere notion of magick, has an affinity with the ways of natural healing and believes in another world of mystical beings. The natural witch is able to connect with this 'other' world, perceiving and working in conjunction with the ancestors, whose wisdom and guidance can be drawn from. This is the way of the witch. A witch is a healer who embraces the workings of nature and takes a responsible attitude in guardianship for our beloved planet and those who reside on it.

Now more than ever you are being urged to awaken the witch within and integrate with the magick and mystery of yesteryear. As you walk along the ancient path of the witch and as an advocate of the old ways you will find freedom to express who you truly are and reclaim your personal power.

The *2025 Witch's Diary* is ideal for any nature lover who wishes to bring the magick of the old ways into their everyday lives. Each month you will discover how to work with specific moon phases and weekdays in order to harness your personal power and enhance your magickal abilities.

This diary is perfect for both the seasoned witch or for those who are exploring the ancient path of the wise. You will find that each page is a magical avenue to draw upon ancient wisdom that is still relevant for the modern witch today.

You'll find each page assists you well
Through incantation, message, spell
Tools explained, history unearthed
Allowing magick to be birthed
The witch in you will be empowered
No more will others leave you soured
Look no further than inside.
It's here the magick doth reside.

Blessed be,
Flavia and Barbara

MOON PHASES

The moon has always fascinated humankind, its luminosity hinting at our celestial origins so it's no wonder the ancients worshipped it as the goddess herself. All things in life are interconnected, so the frequencies emanating from the moon can affect your feelings and emotions. When you become acquainted with the moon's phases you'll know when to cast certain spells and when to access its energies for its particular transformational powers.

~ Dark or old moon ~

This phase is a powerful time to remove and banish things, people or situations, a time to neutralise spells made against others. It is also a potent time for understanding your fears and anger and bringing about justice.

Time of transition from the dark moon to the new moon.

~ Waxing crescent moon ~

This phase is for constructive magic to increase things, fresh beginnings and relationships and for sowing seeds for new ventures. It is the best time to set your intentions for positive outcomes.

~ First quarter moon ~

This phase is the optimum time for drawing things in such as money, success, friends, lovers and work, and for attracting what you most desire into manifestation. It also indicates a period of acceleration and growth.

~ Waxing gibbous moon ~

This phase is about the renewal of strength
and energy. It's a time to focus on willpower
and seeing things through and surrender to and
trust the universe. This is the most powerful
moon phase for fruition and completion.

~ Full moon ~

During a full moon what no longer serves
you will be released and you can harness extra
power to overcome difficult challenges. This is
a time of manifestation, when you can use rituals
and spells for protection and divination and for
healing long-standing illnesses. A full moon is
the most powerful one and its magick is potent.

~ Waning gibbous moon ~

This is a great time to expel all negative thoughts
and influences. Waning moon energies rid and
repel so it is a time to decrease and bring things
to an end, and a time of facing your shadows.

~ Last quarter moon ~

This is a phase of transitions, and for removing
obstacles and avoiding temptations.

~ Waning crescent moon ~

With this phase comes a transition between
the death of the old and the birth of the
new. It's a time of banishment and retreat.

*Between a dark moon and a waxing crescent
moon is a period of stillness called the
new moon, which is the space between
the past and new beginnings. This is a
very powerful phase of transition.*

LUNAR AND SOLAR ECLIPSES

Eclipses are magickal astrological events that can fuel a witch's intentions, wishes and spells with cosmic energy to manifest new beginnings and empowering, positive change.

Solar eclipses occur during a new moon. When the sun, moon and earth are in alignment the moon casts a shadow across the earth that fully or partially blocks out the sun. For witches, a solar eclipse means harnessing the magic of fresh beginnings to truly transform.

A lunar eclipse occurs only during a full moon. When the sun and earth are in close alignment with the moon it moves into the earth's shadow and becomes fully or partially obscured. For witches, a lunar eclipse means harnessing the magick of empowerment and manifestation.

2025

14 March: total lunar eclipse

29 March: partial solar eclipse

7 September: total lunar eclipse

21 September: partial solar eclipse

2026

17 February: annular solar eclipse

3 March: total lunar eclipse

12 August: total solar eclipse

28 August: partial lunar eclipse

FULL MOONS

A full moon usually happens once a month, and when there are two full moons in a month the second one is called a blue moon. During a full moon phase the ability to manifest magick is at its optimum. Each full moon has a variety of names relating to the month and a unique mystical energy that can be harnessed to enhance your own magickal workings.

JANUARY: olde, frost, birch, cold moon.
Letting go of the past and invoking the new.

FEBRUARY: ice, snow, rowan, quickening moon.
The journey of the soul inwards.

MARCH: moon of winds, storm, ash, worm, crow moon.
Coming from the darkness and growing into the light.

APRIL: growing, alder, seed moon.
Growth and the planting of new ideas.

MAY: hare, milk, bright, willow moon.
*Attention to your needs and the
needs of those you love.*

JUNE: moon of horses, hawthorn, strawberry moon.
Balance and understanding.

JULY: hay, thunder, mead, oak moon.
Making plans for the future.

AUGUST: corn, holly, grain moon.
Removing excess baggage and being flexible.

SEPTEMBER: harvest, hazel, fruit, barley moon.
Completion and future prospects.

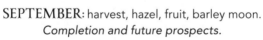

OCTOBER: blood, vine, hunter's moon.
Soul growth and deep inner wisdom.

NOVEMBER: snow, ivy, dark moon.
Truth and honesty while reassessing your life.

DECEMBER: wolf, elder, cold moon.
Healing old wounds and emotions.

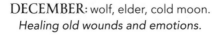

THE WHEEL OF THE YEAR

Spiritual wisdom can be gained by recognising the traditions of old witchcraft and the connection with the seasons. As the witches of old worked with the elemental forces of nature they also honoured the aspects of the triple goddess in relation to the seasons and festivals celebrated through the wheel of the year.

In nature the year is made up of four seasons. The sun marks any seasonal change, and these changes are honoured by celebrating four solar festivals. Fire festivals are marked by cross-quarter and equinox celebrations, so altogether eight festivals of the seasons become the wheel of the year. These festivals represent the state of nature at the time, the agricultural calendar and the physical and spiritual effects the time of year has on humankind.

From planting in spring to harvesting in autumn, the seasons are of great importance. Different celebrations mark times to count your blessings, for reaping and recognising all that you've sown and for giving thanks to nature spirits and the goddess in her triple aspect of maiden, mother and crone as she continues the circle that is called life on earth.

CROSS-QUARTER FESTIVALS AND EQUINOXES

IMBOLC, 1 FEBRUARY: this is a time of fresh growth, as new shoots appear from the ground, early shoots begin to show and the start of the renewal of life is witnessed. The maiden: innocence, purity, seeding the dream and birthing the inner child.

OSTARA, 20 MARCH: this is a time when balance hangs in the air, the length of day equals that of night and the birth of new life is celebrated. The maiden matures: from dark to light we explore signs of growth and discernment.

BELTANE, 1 MAY: this fire festival celebrates the full bloom of nature. The maiden: fertile minds, bodies and souls, birthing your ideas and your soul's knowing.

LITHA, 21 JUNE: this festival celebrates the summer solstice, the longest day of the year. The mother glorified: a celebration of light and being in your full glory.

LUGHNASADH, 1 AUGUST: the time when the grain harvest is cut down and celebrated. The mother matures: gratitude for earthly, physical sustenance.

MABON, 22 SEPTEMBER: during this time day and night are balanced and the fruit harvest is celebrated. The mother: the art of contemplation is explored and there is self-sufficiency of mind, body and spirit.

SAMHAIN, 31 OCTOBER: this is the time to honour the souls of the dead and when the veil between the worlds is at its thinnest. The crone revered: respecting your ancestors and healing your hurts.

YULE, 21 DECEMBER: the winter solstice is a celebration of the rebirth of the sun, for now that the longest night has arrived the days start to grow longer. The crone fades: the returning sun and an exploration of the purest energy that is the essence of your being.

PLANTING AND HARVESTING DAYS

Witches have always planted according to the moon cycles and in conjunction with the movement of the planets, because they understand that different plants grow better when they are planted during different phases of the moon. Each moon phase imparts an influence on the way vegetation grows through the rising and falling of the moisture in the ground and in the plants: how a plant stores water in the fruit/crop at different times of the moon cycle is critical. It's not just planting that is the most important time for the farmer; harvest time also has to be considered, as harvesting at the correct time ensures crops last much longer.

NEW MOON: an excellent time to sow leafy plants such as cabbages, broccoli, celery and cauliflowers and transplant leafy annuals.

WAXING MOON: sap flows and rises, so this is a good time for new growth. Sow or transplant flowering annuals, biennials and grains and plant fruits or flowers that are to be harvested.

FIRST QUARTER MOON: this is the time to plant tomatoes, beets, broccoli, beans and squashes.

FULL MOON: during a full moon sow or plant root crops such as potatoes and asparagus and fruit perennials such as apples and rhubarb. It is the perfect time for separating plants and taking cuttings.

WANING MOON: sap is drawn down during a waning moon, so plant perennials and root crops. It's a good time to prune and harvest.

LAST QUARTER MOON: this is the time to weed, dig or plough and improve the soil with compost or manure.

PLANET RULERS AND SIGNS

Each zodiac sign is affiliated with a planet or celestial body that is said to be its ruler. The ruling planet/celestial body adds dimension and influence to the sign it rules and influences how the sign is expressed, which gives insights into the personality traits intrinsic within the sign.

 ARIES
Mars

 LIBRA
Venus

 TAURUS
Venus

 SCORPIO
Mars

 GEMINI
Mercury

 SAGITTARIUS
Jupiter

 CANCER
The moon

 CAPRICORN
Saturn

 LEO
The sun

 AQUARIUS
Uranus

 VIRGO
Mercury

 PISCES
Neptune

THE GODDESS AND MOON PHASES

The goddess is worshipped in conjunction with the phases of the moon – waxing, full and waning – which represent the three phases of the goddess as maiden, mother and crone.

~ MAIDEN ~

ASPECTS: beauty, enchantment, inception, expansion, new beginnings, youth, excitement, virgin, innocence.

Season: spring.

Colour: white.

Moon phase: waxing.

Festivals: Imbolc, Ostara (spring equinox), Beltane.

~ MOTHER ~

ASPECTS: ripeness, fertility, growth, fulfilment, stability, giving, nurturing, compassion.

Season: summer.

Colour: red.

Moon phase: full.

Festivals: Litha (summer solstice), Lughnasadh, Mabon (autumn equinox).

~ CRONE ~

ASPECTS: wisdom, repose, magic, destruction, decay, death.

Season: winter.

Colour: black.

Moon phases: waning, dark, new.

Festivals: Samhain (Hallowe'en), Yule (winter solstice).

MAGICAL WEEKDAYS

Witches adhere to specific magickal timings such as weekdays to enhance their magickal practice and so they can work with universal energies while they are at their most potent in relation to the chosen spell.

~ SUNDAY ~

The day of the god Apollo, ruled by the sun: this day is imbued with energy and divine guidance and is perfect for relaxing, unwinding and focusing on health and well-being to light up your inner sunshine.

~ MONDAY ~

The day of the goddess Diana, ruled by the moon: this is a day for discovering your true potential and intuition and looking deep within and honouring your emotions.

~ TUESDAY ~

The day of Týr, ruled by Mars: a day for projects, new jobs and decision-making and to take steps to fulfil your dreams, goals and desires.

~ WEDNESDAY ~

The day of the god Woden (Odin), ruled by Mercury: a day to express yourself and focus on life decisions and for communication and messages.

~ THURSDAY ~

The day of the god Thor, ruled by Jupiter: a day of gratitude and positivity and a time of expansion of your mind, body and spirit.

~ FRIDAY ~

The day of the goddess Frigg, ruled by Venus: a day of love and self-care and a time to create and connect with others.

~ SATURDAY ~

The day of the god Saturn: a great day to tackle big projects and be responsible and get organised both at home and at work. It's also a time to be grounded and balanced.

MAGICAL MOON TIMES
TO CAST SPELLS

~ DARK MOON ~
from dawn to sunset.

~ WAXING CRESCENT MOON ~
from mid-morning until after sunset.

~ FIRST QUARTER MOON ~
from noon until midnight.

~ WAXING GIBBOUS MOON ~
from mid-afternoon until 3.00 am.

~ FULL MOON ~
from sunset until dawn.

~ WANING GIBBOUS MOON ~
from mid-evening until mid-morning.

~ LAST QUARTER MOON ~
from midnight until noon.

~ WANING CRESCENT MOON ~
from 3.00 am until mid-afternoon.

MAGICKAL MEANINGS OF COLOURS

Colour is a natural source of cosmic energy that a witch can draw upon. Every colour has its own unique vibration and resonance, which can be harnessed for magickal spells and healing and used in the form of, for example, coloured candles, cloth or crystals.

~ BLACK ~
elimination, banishment, retribution, north, earth.

~ BLUE ~
peace, harmony, healing, curing fevers, reuniting friendships, house blessings.

~ BROWN ~
grounding, stabilisation, intuition, balance, connection with Mother Earth.

~ GOLD ~
cosmic influences, solar deities, success, wealth, influence.

~ GREEN ~
fertility, good fortune, generosity, wealth, success, renewal, marriage, healing.

~ INDIGO ~
meditation, balancing karma, stopping gossip, astral projection.

~ MAGENTA ~
rapid change, spiritual healing, exorcism.

~ ORANGE ~
communication, telepathy, new job, adaptability, luck, control, attraction.

~ PINK ~
romance, affection, love, spiritual awakening, unity.

~ PURPLE ~
honour, respect, wisdom, divine knowing, trust, spiritual connection.

~ SILVER ~
moon magic, protection from entities, inner peace, serenity.

~ WHITE ~
purification, blessings, aspect of light, cosmos.

MAGICKAL DIRECTIONS AND ELEMENTS

Each direction is assigned to one of the four basic elements of earth, air, fire and water; without them this planet would be lifeless. The four basic elements work in harmony with each other and with the fifth element of spirit, which runs through everything to create and sustain life. Each of the four basic elements is associated with a direction, a season and a moon phase when it comes to magickal workings, and we acknowledge above, below and within. Witches work naturally with the forces of nature, and call upon the guardians of each direction when creating sacred space and before ritual and spell casting.

~ NORTH ~

the element of earth and the season of winter;
a time of the new moon and midnight.

~ WEST ~

the element of water and the season of autumn; *a time of the waning moon and dusk.*

~ EAST ~

the element of air and the season of spring; *a time of the waxing moon and sunrise.*

~ SOUTH ~

the element of fire and the season of summer; *a time of the full moon and noon.*

~ ABOVE ~

mind connection with the universal great mystery.

~ BELOW ~

body connection with the earth.

~ WITHIN ~

spirit connection with your inner universe, the great void.

TREES OF POWER

Ancient and enduring and known as the standing ones, trees are wisdom keepers and mystical gateways to the otherworld. Trees have long been associated with witches, for they hold the magickal secrets of yesteryear and are extreme sources of power a witch can draw upon. The spirits of the trees are multidimensional and they each have their own magickal properties.

ALDER: resurrection, rebirth, fire.

APPLE: healing, prosperity, love,
peace, happiness, youth.

ASH: healing, protection, sea magic.

BIRCH: new beginnings and births, fertility,
purification, protection, blessings.

BLACKTHORN: bad luck, strife, unexpected
changes, death, wounding, curses.

CEDAR: purification, prosperity, longevity;
represents the earth and spirituality.

ELDER: healing, love, protection, prosperity; used to make magickal wands.

ELM: primordial female powers, protection.

FIR: youth, vitality; used in prosperity magick.

HAWTHORN: female sexuality, cleansing, marriage, love, protection; a magickal tool.

HAZEL: fertility, divination, marriage, protection, reconciliation; used to make wands.

HOLLY: protection.

OAK: healing, strength, longevity.

PINE: immortality, fertility, health, prosperity; represents the earth.

ROWAN: protection, healing, strength; represents fire.

WILLOW: moon and wishing magic, healing, protection, enchantments; represents water.

YEW: immortality, rebirth, protection, longevity, change, divinity, strength.

TREE INCANTATION

Wisdom keepers standing tall
From roots to branches, hear their call
Magickally drawn to meditate
Connect within; don't hesitate!
Against a trunk: sit, lean and feel
Powerfully charged to ground and heal.

DANU

JANUARY

Olde, frost, birch, cold moon

Letting go of the past and invoking the new

The month of January brings the energy of a new start as the calendar year begins. In the northern hemisphere the cold, hard earth remains steeped in deep magick and mystery, nurturing and restoring all that resides within it and offering comfort from the hardships the glacial callousness of winter brings. The goddess is in her crone phase but she is beginning to fade as the promise of new life beckons, and the days are getting longer since her deathly reign of winter and the solstice at Yule. This is a time of a slow awakening for all of nature and to look at setting different goals as you leave old regrets behind and make fresh resolutions through intention, ritual and spells to assist you through the coming months and warmer days.

It's time to take the first brave steps of authenticity toward the magickal freedom of embracing the witch within, to stop hesitating and hiding in the shadows. Bid farewell to negativity, control and disempowerment and embrace the lessons of the past, as the door closes on yesteryear and brighter experiences await. The crone offers you rebirth and transformation as you follow the wheel of the year and the magick of the old ways.

GODDESS: **Danu (Celtic/Irish),** first great mother, earth goddess, cosmic triple goddess.

CRONE: transformation, dreams, clarity, wisdom, alchemical magick.

MOON MAGICK

The darkness of winter may have shrouded your light. Be careful as you further explore the darker recesses of the self not to be consumed by the tortuous depths of your mind. As you feel the pull of the cold moon, self-criticism, frustration and depression may seek you out and reveal the past, old fights and memories that repeat over and over. Perverting your divinity will keep you locked in deep despair, where you will remain powerless, so be wary of letting the deafening silence of self-blame or guilt spiral out of control. The cold moon of January invites you to go deep within and surrender, to learn to venerate yourself with witchy reverence, dignity and honour. Remember that it is only from out of the dark that light can be birthed, and soon you shall be restored with the returning light.

COLD MOON

Desolation of cold moon
Darkened thoughts of gloom and doom
Feel the pull, go deep within
Surrender if you wish to win
This moon magick is said and done
So mote it be, with harm to none.

RITUAL MAGICK

Light a black candle and place it down carefully.
Raise your arms to the moon and say:

I welcome you and all you bring
Fears to face, journey within
Now ready for a witch's death
New life poised upon my breath.

Allow the recalibration to reveal the light within the darkness. Acknowledge and honour the cycle of death and rebirth and snuff out the candle. A new year awaits!

30 Monday

31 Tuesday

1 Wednesday

Between 40,000 to 50,000 executions occurred after witch-hunts between 1450 and 1750.
Not all witch-hunts were recorded, so an accurate number of executions cannot be arrived at.

2 Thursday

3 Friday

4 Saturday

Doreen Valiente (1922-99), mother of modern witchcraft, United Kingdom.

5 Sunday

Barbara Meiklejohn-Free (1957–), elder, high priestess, highland seer and occultist, United Kingdom.

6 Monday
First quarter moon.

7 Tuesday

8 Wednesday
Samuel Liddell MacGregor Mathers (1854–1918), co-founder of the Hermetic Order of the Golden Dawn, London, United Kingdom.

9 Thursday

10 Friday

11 Saturday
The trial of the Basque witches began in January 1609 in Logroño, Spain.

12 Sunday

WITCHY TIP

It's time to step out of the broom closet and reveal your true authentic self, for you can no longer hide the truth of who you are for fear of being persecuted. Instead, the depth of your witchy soul urges you to take the first brave steps of authenticity, to have the freedom to live the life you crave as the real magickal you.

OUT OF THE BROOM CLOSET

With a clean sweep and tickle of brush
No longer should you keep hush hush
From out of the closet, take a stance
No need to hide; for now's your chance
To live your life, claim who you are
Shout 'I'm a witch!' Become the star.

KITCHEN WITCHERY

MANDRAKE: at this time of year your spirit may have waned and your sparkle dimmed. However, all is not lost, as a new magick surrounds you when I appear for no other plant has been more associated with or respected by witches through the ages as I. A magickal alliance has been made between witches and the spirit of Mandragora, and my root is used as a vessel for familiars to feed from. In return I am fed with milk or wine under a dark moon. Be sure not to feed on me yourself, though, for I will cause delirium or even madness if ingested much like my poisonousness cousin belladonna. Instead, use my powdered root wisely as a magickal catalyst to empower amulets, spells and fertility rituals, and to induce visions and free your spirit. Your much desired freedom of magickal expression is waiting to be unearthed.

MANDRAKE: IMPASSIVE

Magick's waned, not impressed
Work with my root if you're distressed
Extraction causes deadly scream
Work with me to follow your dream
Mandrake magick is worked with harm to none
So mote it be; there, it is done.

13 Monday
Full moon.

14 Tuesday

15 Wednesday

16 Thursday

17 Friday

18 Saturday

19 Sunday
In Valais, Switzerland 367 people were condemned for practising witchcraft from 1428 to 1448.

JANUARY

20 Monday

21 Tuesday
Third quarter moon.

22 Wednesday
In Trier, Germany 368 people were condemned for practising witchcraft from 1581 to 1593.

23 Thursday

24 Friday
Theoris of Lemnos (fourth century BCE), Greek witch and folk healer, was executed.

25 Saturday

26 Sunday

Draw in your mind a five-pointed
star in front of you. Step into it and pour
a circle of salt around you to make a pentacle.
Hold a lit black candle in one hand as you face
the direction of north and a grounding piece of
black tourmaline crystal in your other hand and say:

Pentagram star in a circle of salt
Protection in place from any default
Shield me, guard me, from hazards and hurt
From gossip and curses, from dishing the dirt
Surrounded by the elements, five
Resolutions defended; this year I'll survive
Resisting is futile, I'll no longer fight.
With focus, intentions, I look to the light
Standing within, I lift up my arms
Positive purpose now banishes harm
Safe to reclaim my new witchy flow
While raising vibration the mystery doth grow
I stand in my power, protection in place
Magick and ritual now safe to embrace.

Blow out the black candle and carefully step out
of the circle. Bury the black tourmaline under
the cold moon to restore, recharge and reclaim
your magick and power as a witch. Say:

Gratefully I accept the magick of you
Of protection to assist in all that I do
Lend me the courage, build power in me
Assist my transcendence. So mote it be.

NEW YEAR SPELL

BRIDGET

FEBRUARY

Ice, snow, rowan, quickening moon
A time of purification and hope

After the harshness of winter, this is a time of emergence as new shoots appear from the ground, early flowers begin to blossom and the start of the renewal of life is witnessed. Daylight hours finally become noticeably longer and the birth of the very first lambs as the ewes start to lactate is celebrated. It was an important time for our ancestors as fresh milk once again became available, meaning the difference between life and death after the cold, harsh scarcity of winter.

IMBOLC: 1 FEBRUARY

GODDESS: **Bridget (Irish/Celtic),** new life, hope, growth.

MAIDEN: innocence, purity, seeding the dream.

IMBOLC
First signs of new growth

At Imbolc it is traditional to pour fresh milk on the ground to honour Mother Earth and ensure fertility for the coming season. In agriculture, this is when seeds are planted and signs of flowers such as snowdrops and crocuses starting to grow can be seen. Imbolc is a time of purification in preparation for the coming year and is portrayed as the young virgin maiden aspect of the Celtic triple goddess. She is the young girl awakening to womanhood just as nature begins its fertility cycle and offers us new life and fresh beginnings.

This is the time to seed your new ideas, to make plans and begin creative projects that will grow into fruition through the warmer months to come. As nature starts to wake up it's time to plant and seed your wishes and desires, to awaken and create different dreams and goals.

Witchy recipe

This mandrake ritual extract is great for the home, ritual magick, empowering spells and your altar and tools. Slice mandrake root and add it to a glass jar. Steep for three moon cycles, beginning at the dark of the moon. Cover the jar with a black cloth and store in a dark place, ensuring the jar is labelled and only used in ritual. Set your intention and speak with the spirit of mandrake before use.

Witch's wisdom

The witch within urges you to re-awaken; determination and focus will drive your desires into fruition. As you step into alignment through spell work, invocation and acknowledging the aspects of both your light and shadow sides you will become testimony to the wise ones who walked before you. January's moon is poised to support you as it reflects your intentions, so go grab your dreams and reach for your goals as the magick of the new year surges through you. Everything is yours for the taking: wise up and add your own magickal sprinkling to the year ahead.

Witchy tip

Use the five-pointed pentagram symbol for magickal protection. Keep your secrets close to your chest and work as a solitary. Guard yourself from negative energies and add safety precautions to your home. It's time to defend your honour and beliefs, and to put family protection first.

27 Monday

28 Tuesday

Agnes Sampson, midwife, was strangled then burned as a witch in 1591 in Royal Mile, Edinburgh. Her trial was the start of all the witch trials to come in Scotland.

29 Wednesday

New moon.

30 Thursday

The persecution of witches in Rome continued until the late fourth century CE.

31 Friday

1 Saturday

Imbolc · Persecution of the Cathars in France around 1450 for witchcraft and heresy.

2 Sunday

FEBRUARY

3   Monday

4   Tuesday

5   Wednesday

First quarter moon · Janet Horne was the last woman in the United Kingdom to be legally executed for practising witchcraft, in 1727.

6   Thursday

7   Friday

8   Saturday

Éliphas Lévi Zahed, greatest occultist of the 19th century.

9   Sunday

IMBOLC INCANTATION

'Neath a layer of soft white snow
Doth a single flower grow
The goddess stands in maiden form
Shining through this very dawn
New fruits stir her virgin womb
Awakening from winter's tomb
She calls to you to be free
Explore each possibility
For now is when to seed your dreams
No matter how hard and tough life seems
They will come true; it's time to trust
Be one with nature, don't fight or thrust
Take the cup she offers you
That's filled with milk from a ewe
Embrace the year through open eyes
Magick awaits; nature tells no lies.

─────────○─────────

WITCH'S WISDOM

The triple goddess in her maiden form invites you greet her at a pure level, to reclaim the innocent part within that nourishes, fills you and reminds you to focus as you set new goals. It's necessary to return to simplicity, to release rigidity and ideas of perfection. Instead, as you forge new intentions honour your maiden qualities of beauty and innocence and the imaginative part of you that fuels your creative spark, your inner child who just wants to have fun, lighten up and splash about in puddles. February's snow moon shines upon you as the maiden beckons you to play under its soft lunar glow. As all of nature awakens with every bright step she takes across the risen land, it is time to discover all the fresh offerings of spring. A glimmer of hope sparkles in the moonlight, indicating fresh ideas, beginnings and golden opportunities. The maiden offers you a clean slate, so purify your thoughts, actions and diet, too, for this is a time of new growth as you seed fresh ideas. It is time to arise!

─────────○─────────

SNOW MOON:
PURIFICATION

'Neath a layer of soft white snow
Doth a single flower grow
Purify to cleanse, be free
Enhancing spirituality
This moon magick is said and done
So mote it be, with harm to none.

MOON MAGICK

Hiding behind magickal artefacts and a witchy exterior doesn't make a witch. Stale energies block desired intentions and prevent magickal outcomes. When your energy is clogged with guilt, blame, fears and impure substances it's time for a little witchy purification. Engage in purifying ritual to purge and cleanse, and allow the power of purification to lift the energy around your hearth, home and altar and purify unwanted vibrational energies of the past. As your working space becomes ceremonially cleansed you are offered a clean slate that will raise you to a higher frequency, promoting fresh ideas and nurturing your maiden qualities of awe and wonder as you play under the soft glow of the full snow moon. Allow all rigidity to release as ideas of perfection melt away.

FEBRUARY

10 Monday

11 Tuesday

12 Wednesday

Full moon · To date more than 15,000 children from the ages of newborn to two have been abandoned and branded as witches and left to die on the streets of Nigeria. Outdated religious beliefs that children are evil and possessed by bad spirits are the cause of this atrocity, which is still happening today.

13 Thursday

14 Friday

15 Saturday

16 Sunday

Pamela Colman Smith (1878-1951), occultist and artist of the Rider-Waite Tarot.

17 Monday

18 Tuesday

19 Wednesday

More than 5,000 members of the Bacchus cult were executed between 182 and 184 BCE by the Roman senate for practising witchcraft at the ecstatic rites of Dionysus.

20 Thursday

Third quarter moon.

21 Friday

22 Saturday

La Voisin (1640–80), French fortune-teller, sorceress and commissioned poisoner, burned at the stake. Sybil Leek (1917–82), witch, occult author and astrologer.

23 Sunday

RITUAL MAGICK

To purify your energy, waft the smoke of Californian white sage or an incense stick over your head and body. Imagine etheric flames purging through your body to purify and transmute any dross, raising your vibration. Cleanse and clean in the shower, visualising golden purifying light washing over you. Bury yourself in the earth to rejuvenate, tone high-frequency chants for purification and say blessings.

FAMILIAR'S MESSAGE

BROWNIE: creaky floorboards, spooky sounds and ghostly whispers are not comforting night-time companions, and vulnerability from the actions of others may have left you feeling threatened.

As guardian of your hearth and home, invite me to cross your threshold and I shall protect all that is sacred to you. As I employ a little brownie magick in a non-confrontational manner I offer to be eternally helpful if you allow me to go quietly about my business. As I watch in the dead of night over the burning home fires and complete unfinished tasks, you can rest in your bed safely assured as I create protective barriers to drive away unwelcome visitors and safeguard your secrets. However, treat me badly or try to assist me and I will sharply leave or turn into a malicious boggart!

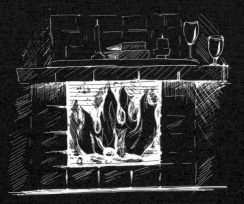

BROWNIE MAGICK: PROTECTION

Invitation to work through the night
Tasks to complete when out of sight
Protection in place, secrets to keep
Within hearth and home, safe now to sleep.

BROWNIES

Brownies protect what is sacred to you, from your home and family to your beliefs. Work with brownie magick to keep something under the radar: leave a bowl of cream by the hearth as an offering. Brownies don't like to be seen, nor do they accept help or praise in return for their household chores, and they will walk away if they are insulted.

24 Monday

Urbain Grandier (1590–1634), a priest of the Church of Sainte Croix in western France, wasburned alive for bewitching the nuns by sending the devil to seduce them. Grandier was charged with witchcraft and tortured by the extraordinary question, a form of torture used on the condemned. He never broke his word.

25 Tuesday

Forty-five men and 85 women suspected of sorcery were executed during the reign of Tiberius Claudius, from 41 to 54 CE.

26 Wednesday

27 Thursday

Comte de Saint Germain (1712–84), Hungarian alchemist and philosopher.

28 Friday

New moon · The first warrants were issued at the Salem witch trials on 29 February 1692.

1 Saturday

First Witchcraft Act in England in 1542; the instigator was Henry VIII. The witch trials in Salem began in 1692.

2 Sunday

WITCHY TIP

Restriction and control can dim your spirit and suffocate the expression of your witchy soul. Remember you have been gifted with free will, so rise openly above anything that has enslaved or imprisoned you and allow your loaded mind to be liberated as your heart and soul soar to new heights. At this time of year, make your wishes and set your goals to grow into fruition through the coming months.

FREEDOM SPELL

Stand under the moon while holding a feather
to place your wishes into and say:

Soul doth stir from prison deep
Confinement fades; it's not to keep
Prisoner of mind and actions
Relationships add to fractions
Wishes made for liberation
Place in feather to awaken
Throw in air upon the breeze
Restrictions lifted now with ease
Stars determine destiny
Mine to claim for liberty.

Throw the feather up to the stars:
freedom has been granted!

MARCH

Moon of winds, storm, ash, worm, crow moon
Coming from the darkness and growing into the light

In like a lion and out like a lamb, the winds of change welcome in this wild month with its hope of warmer days to come. The energy at this waxing time of year becomes expansive as the light grows strong enough to defeat the dark, and the natural world comes alive as the sun gains strength with the promise of longer days. As the goddess in her maiden form walks across the land, all of nature wakes up to the fulfilled promises made at Imbolc as she breathes new life into the world. Spring has sprung!

OSTARA: 20 March

GODDESS: **Ēostre/Ostara (Anglo/Germanic),**
of spring, fertility, renewal, fruitfulness.

MAIDEN: the dark of the old aligns with new
light, signs of growth, creative power.

OSTARA

Alignment of the natural world

Ostara heralds the spring equinox, a time of balance between light and dark and a day of equilibrium. When you are aligned with the natural world you can embrace and honour the fresh creative power that is stirring throughout nature.

Ostara is a time for honouring new life and is the festival that was borrowed from age-old traditions to become Easter: think hatched eggs, baby chicks, moon-gazing hares and all the fresh promises of spring. Call upon the spirits of the air to enhance your creativity and meditation abilities and stimulate your mind as you light incense and a yellow candle and face the direction of east. This is a great time for fertility as air blows you in the direction of fresh beginnings, so throw caution to the wind and watch as your visions manifest into reality.

Ostara incantation

Celebrate the stirring of spring
Natural balance doth it bring
Claim that of which it represents
New life, growth and expectance
Seeds planted in nature's tomb
Incubate within her womb
Symbolic hares upon the lawn
Herald the goddess of the dawn
And from the east the sun doth rise
Shining bright across the skies
The goddess works behind the scenes
To manifest your goals and dreams
Await and trust now; 'tis the key
For life will bloom most readily.

3 Monday

4 Tuesday

Lilias Adie (1640-1704), Scottish witch, died in prison before her sentence was passed. She is the only witch in Scotland to have a grave, at Torryburn Bay in intertidal mud and with a heavy stone doorstep on top.

5 Wednesday

6 Thursday

First quarter moon · Laurie Cabot (1933-), high priestess and occultist, Salem, United States.

7 Friday

8 Saturday

International Women's Day. On this day in 2022 Nicola Sturgeon, a Scottish first minister, offered a formal apology and pardon to all of the 2,558 women and men who had been convicted of witchcraft and executed between 1563 and 1736.

9 Sunday

Between the fourth and sixth centuries CE more than 1,000 witches were persecuted and expelled from the Huns, a nomadic tribe.

10 Monday

11 Tuesday

12 Wednesday

Hypatia (350–415), ancient philosopher and astronomer, murdered by a Christian mob that had accused her of practising witchcraft.

13 Thursday

14 Friday

Full moon, total lunar eclipse.

15 Saturday

16 Sunday

WITCH'S WISDOM

When the element of air blows through the power of your mind, all visions, dreams and insights are richly enhanced and you are urged to believe that what you see within is indeed real. Take a moment to focus on the sacred space within, for reflection to nourish your creative spirit and expand your imagination. Imagination is the secret portal to the otherworld: it really is the gateway to magick! When you close your eyes, vivid colours or pictures, repetitive signs and symbols are confirmed as magickal messages, for it is a time of new life, of different possibilities carried upon the four winds that breathe forth your thoughts and dreams into this reality and dimension. All you need do is trust what you see and believe.

IMAGINATION INCANTATION

Air blows in with all its might
Illuminating sacred sight
Visions, dreams: trust to see
Imagination is the key.

RITUAL MAGICK

The magick of air stimulates the power of your mind, enhances your intellect and brings about mental clarity. Light a yellow candle and face east under the new pink moon on 29 March. Place your intention to enhance imagination into a feather and throw it to ride upon the east wind into new beginnings.

Familiar's Message

BLACKBIRD: Omens, signs and symbols await manifestation within your world of vision. I will guide you on your personal journey between the worlds so you may rediscover the mystical meaning of your premonitions. You are an old soul, carrying shrouded secrets within. Many do not understand you because you are different, a solitary ridiculed by those who do not understand your way of life. It is time to step into the unknown and discover a whole new world that awaits. No longer will you be hidden in the shadows, but out in the open with your newfound voice. Words have power as you embrace your omens and visions with clarity and determination. With steadfast courage and resilience don't just 'wing it'. It's time to sing your soul back home.

Blackbird: omens

Where a blackbird be, omens all around
Songs in shadows, dead of night, listen to the sound
Hidden secret messages, mystical signs, rife
Point toward the future to make magickal your life.

17 Monday

18 Tuesday

Manly Palmer Hall (1901–90), mystic and astrologer.

19 Wednesday

20 Thursday

Ostara, spring equinox.

21 Friday

22 Saturday

Third quarter moon.

23 Sunday

In the 1590s Scottish King James I's fear of witchcraft and black magic caused thousands of witches, mostly women, to be burned and tortured. He believed there was a witchcraft conspiracy against him that threatened his reign.

24 Monday

25 Tuesday

26 Wednesday

Zhang Liang, who fought for China's Tang Dynasty, was the first person in recorded history to be executed for witchcraft, in 646 CE.

27 Thursday

28 Friday

29 Saturday

New moon, partial solar eclipse · Granny Boswell (1817–1909), well-known local witch in Cornwall; married the king of the witches.

30 Sunday

BLACKBIRD WITCHY TIPS

The gift of three feathers to another reveals hidden secrets. Visions of a blackbird in dreamwork warn of forthcoming dangers. A flying blackbird in dreams signifies good luck. Placing a feather in one's hair strengthens intuition and assists in spell-casting. The goddess Rhiannon's familiars are three magical blackbirds who assist seekers in gaining access to magical secrets.

GODDESS GUIDANCE

RHIANNON: allow the light of the moon and stars to let ancient memories stir within as we ride together swiftly through the night upon my white horse. As the moon streams its sacred light, feel the force field of silver inviting you to expand your awareness of dream recall and astral travel. A newfound awareness and perception will open doors to many realms as you pay attention to dreams. Keep a journal and explore lucid dreaming as you meet old loved ones in the dreamtime. Everything is limitless, including *you*!

LUCID DREAMING INCANTATION

Dreams are healed, nightmares taken
A kiss is sealed; time to awaken
Memories stir, travel awaits
Look to the stars, trust in the fates.

RITUAL MAGICK

To enhance lucid dreaming, shower with lavender oil
and place moonstone under your pillow. Scratch your
intention on a white candle, light it and safely burn
it down. Clear your mind, relax and repeat:

Tonight in my dreams I am fully aware
I'm fully protected, there's nothing to scare
Tonight as I sleep, there is no need to scream
I am dreaming awake and aware of the dream.

LAVENDER: SWEET DREAMS

Worries or stress won't help you sleep
But a pinch of me will take you deep
Inhale my scent before you go to bed
Then wake refreshed with a clear head
This magick is worked, with harm to none
So mote it be; there, it is done.

KITCHEN WITCHERY

LAVENDER POUCH: use this pouch to
help combat insomnia and aid sleep. Craft
a sachet bag or purchase an organza bag and
fill it with dried-out lavender flower buds. Add
a couple of drops of pure lavender essential
oil if you'd like a stronger scent. Tie or sew the
top of the pouch and pop under your pillow
or leave it on your nightstand to ensure
a good night's sleep.

NEW BEGINNINGS SPELL

Hold a pouch of lavender under the moonlight and say:

Call down the moon to reflect the sun
Invoking a life spell that can't be undone
A path that is new, to be revealed
Focus and follow, for fate has been sealed
Lavender flowers, relaxing and calm
Make as a spritz or in a pouch as a balm
Destiny's signposts now point the way
Dreams to embrace, go seize them today.

Write down all that you wish to be, place it in a lavender pouch and pop it under your pillow. Your dreams will soon grow into fruition.

APRIL

Growing, alder, seed moon

Growth planting and connecting with the magic of nature

The fresh, light rain of April brings with it new ideas and inspiration. This is a great time for wishes and magick as the earth springs forth and faeries tend to and nurture their wards, the newly growing flowers. For thousands of years witches and healers have worked alongside the power of the fae, who have shared ancient knowledge of healing herbs, cures and ointments with those who visit their mystical world. As a magickal energy of growth surrounds you the faeries are poised to support you, as heartfelt wishes reflect your thoughts and good intentions. The fae are the guardians of nature who remind you that magick is everywhere and in everything, so go outside and discover it! Enjoy every precious moment, knowing and appreciating that you are totally blessed as you feel the faery witch within stir deeply.

———————————○———————————

GODDESS: **Cordelia (Celtic/British),** faery queen of flowers, faeries, beauty, wishes.

MAIDEN: renewing of spirit, inhaling fresh air, the fragrance of spring flowers.

31 Monday

1 Tuesday

Second Witchcraft Act in England in 1563; the instigator was Elizabeth I.

2 Wednesday

3 Thursday

4 Friday

5 Saturday

First quarter moon.

6 Sunday

After 329 years, the last of the Salem witches was pardoned in 2022. The memorial for those who were executed is situated in Liberty Street, Salem, and opposite the memorial are the gravestones of the witch trial magistrates who condemned them.

7 Monday

Anne Pedersdotter (ca 1530–90), Norwegian witch, burned to death.

8 Tuesday

9 Wednesday

10 Thursday

11 Friday

12 Saturday

Raven Grimassi (1951–2019), high priest, occultist and Wiccan; popularised Stregheria, the root of witchcraft.

13 Sunday

Full moon · William Quan Judge (1851–96), occultist, mystic and founder of the Theosophical Society.

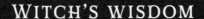

WITCH'S WISDOM

Those who hear the call of nature can feel their mystic self stir from deep within. Glimmers of ancient memories surface, recalling moonlight bathing in deep blue pools. April calls you to weave through forests, feeling the new warmth of the sun as it beams through the budding green leaves of the trees. To the elementals it was only yesterday when they played with you, and they miss you and the magick you exude when you allow yourself to be the free spirit you naturally are. The earth needs your help and the fae are calling you to harness the power of nature, to honour and revere the ways of the witches who worked in union with these very real nature spirits. When you recognise that it is the elementals who are the magick behind all that is alive on this wondrous planet and who work in conjunction with the elements that govern each and every one of us you are brought back into alignment with the natural world. In return they offer you their assistance so that you too can heal, create and thrive in the very modern world in balance and harmony.

FAERY
MAGICK

Faeries are made up of a high-vibrating energy of light and resonate at a greater energy frequency than yours. However, faeries can freely appear to you by slowing down their vibrations. At certain times of the day, such as at the magical hours of sunrise, dusk, noon and midnight, you are more likely to see faeries. Portals from this world to theirs exist through water pools, at the crossings of ancient paths and from circles of mushrooms or flowers.

GARDEN MAGICK

As you sow dreams and tend to your own plot you never need to stray far from the garden gate when choosing cures for ailments or ingredients for magical recipes. Dig deep within and unearth your natural affinity with the world of flora and fauna. As you listen to the subtle messages of wisdom that the plant world emits, allow the deep medicinal properties to restore your healing and love connection with Mother Earth.

GARDEN INCANTATION

Flowers and herbs, grasses and plants
Faery dust sprinkled o'er to enhance
Nurturing phases, cyclical growth
Faery magick, important for both
Sow of the dream, planting each seed
Cultivate all; assured to succeed.

14 Monday

15 Tuesday

During the Channel Island witch trials from 1550 to 1650 more than 100 people were accused, tortured and executed.

16 Wednesday

17 Thursday

18 Friday

King Olaf Tryggvason of Norway (reigned 995-1000 CE) lured more than 100 pagan magicians into his hall under false pretences and accused them of practising witchcraft. The doors were barred and they were burned; those who escaped were captured and drowned.

19 Saturday

20 Sunday

APRIL

21 Monday

Third quarter moon · One of the first regions in Europe to carry out witch hunts was Catalonia in Spain; more than 700 women were tortured and put to death. In 2022 the Catalan parliament formally pardoned the witches after being inspired by the Scottish pardon.

22 Tuesday

23 Wednesday

Ursulines de Jésus (??-1754) was burned to death in Brazil for practising witchcraft.

24 Thursday

25 Friday

26 Saturday

27 Sunday

New moon.

WITCHERY

Even though a faery garden is associated with the element of earth, it is important when working with nature to honour the four basic elements of earth, air, fire and water in some way. Each element works from a different mood and energy:

EARTH: creates the energy of stability, support, and firm grounding.

AIR: governs the feelings of independence, freedom and vitality.

FIRE: increases enthusiasm and passion.

WATER: instils harmony, inner peace and tranquillity.

By balancing these elements a harmonious space can be created for your garden and home. You may wish to add the following to your faery garden:

WIND CHIMES: the high frequency resonance will attract the spirits of air and keep lower-vibrational energy away.

ROCKERY: a rockery will invite in grounded earth energy. Pretty it up with some shiny crystals.

WATER feature: a fountain or pond will add an element of refreshment and relaxation.

FIRE PIT: a stone or cast-iron fire pit will augment the fire element.

WITCHY TIP

Don't be surprised if beautiful-coloured dragonflies turn up and frogs appear to serenade you with the sounds of their croaks, for these creatures have strong links with the faery realm and heal Mother Earth purposefully with the tonal sounds and energies they naturally emit.

FAERY GUIDE SPELL

At the faery magickal time of dusk, gaze into
a mirror and set your intentions by saying:

*Mirror, mirror, give me sight
Show me shadows through the light
Reveal the fae who guard me well
That we might meet through cast of spell
Accept, I shall, new magick in me
Mirror, mirror, let me see.*

Light a white candle and gaze into the flame. Breathe deeply, in and out, through your heart centre. Look into a mirror and watch as the flame dances in its reflection: soon an image of your faery guide, who is ready to transform you into your magickal self, will appear.

28 Monday

29 Tuesday

Titus Livius recorded that 170 women had been executed as witches for causing an epidemic illness in Rome in 331 BCE.

30 Wednesday

1 Thursday

Beltane, May Day.

2 Friday

Third Witchcraft Act in England in 1604; the instigator was James I.

3 Saturday

4 Sunday

First quarter moon.

MAY

Hare, milk, bright, willow moon
A celebration of nature in full bloom

The merry month of May is a celebration of when the energies of nature are at their strongest. All of life is bursting with potent fertility, the goddess is seeded by the god and we witness the conception of new life bursting forth into full bloom at the start of the summer months to come.

BELTANE: 1 May

GODDESS: Blodeuwedd (Celtic/Welsh),
flower face, springtime flowers, new warmth.

MAIDEN: in her fullness, sexuality, sensuality, passion, vitality, consummation.

With fires lit across the land
A couple leaps while hand in hand
To mark their union and this rite
For they know tonight's the night
As they run through darkened wood
And find a grassy glade, they should
Remember well of who's around
For bands of faeries all surround
The couple as they consummate
The faeries cheer and seal the fate
Of plants and flowers, shrubs and trees
While the god's upon his knees
Impregnating the mother to be
From sowing deep his natural seed
And so in time the goddess will birth
The magick that is nature on this earth.

BELTANE INCANTATION

BELTANE

The maiden has
reached her fullness and
is the manifestation of growth,
sexuality, sensuality, passion, vitality
and consummation

Beltane is an age-old, yearly pagan celebration that continues to this day. Villagers gather to eat together and sup ale as they are treated to traditional Morris dancing and a May queen is chosen. Local children weave ribbons in and out as they dance around a decorated maypole. This represents the traditional rituals once held to promote fertility for livestock and people alike.

Traditionally, Beltane is a time of the blending of energies of the feminine and masculine to celebrate the sacredness of sexuality. The goddess takes on the god as her lover in order to give birth to the full bloom of nature during the summer months to come. Beltane marks the return of full life and nature is fully honoured in the fresh bright flowers, grasses and leaves that have started to push through. It is an abundant time of year: think maypoles – a phallic symbol that represents the potency of the gods – May queens, flower garlands, handfasting and hawthorn (known as the May tree) and the lord and lady of the Greenwood.

Beltane is celebrated as a fire festival to honour the Celtic sun god Bel. Great fires blazed from the hilltops as a sign of protection and others were lit for couples to leap over hand in hand before running into the woods to consummate their union. It's a time when goals that were set at the beginning of the year come to fruition, and when projects take off and relationships bloom. Seeds are sown at Beltane and the goddess from her union with her consort gives birth to goals, dreams and ideas, which spring into reality and continue to grow and blossom into fruition.

5 **Monday**

6 **Tuesday**

Margaret Read (??-1590) was burned at the stake in King's Lynn, Norfolk.

7 **Wednesday**

8 **Thursday**

9 **Friday**

Isobel Gowdie (1632-1662), Scottish witch, confessed under duress to practising witchcraft and was most likely executed, although this is unknown for sure.

10 **Saturday**

11 **Sunday**

12 Monday
Full moon.

13 Tuesday
In the first century CE, 80 women were executed for practising witchcraft in Ashkelon in Canaan in the Middle East.

14 Wednesday

15 Thursday
More than 500 witches were executed in England between 1566 and 1700 for the crime of practising witchcraft, and although it has been more 300 years since their deaths there has still been no pardon. In 1998 a pardon was prevented from going through parliament for the Pendle witches.

16 Friday

17 Saturday
Nicholas Culpeper (1616-54), the people's herbalist, botanist, physician and astrologer, was accused of practising witchcraft. He dedicated himself to healing the sick and poor, and his book *Culpeper's Complete Herbal* is still in print.

18 Sunday
Cassandra Latham-Jones (no birth records) was the first person in the United Kingdom to register her work as a witch with the Inland Revenue Department, in 1996.

WITCHY TIP

May is a fertile time; phallic symbols point toward sexual union. Be free, wild and promiscuous and never ashamed of your sexuality. Acknowledge urges and bring them into balance.

HORNED GOD

His breath on your neck will send shivers down your spine, making your pulse race in a frenzied desire to become one with the wild essence of the sacred patriarchal divine who awakens and unleashes your own animal magnetism potency and the innermost desires, lusts and fantasies you dare not admit to the world. However, the horned and horny god knows your innermost sacred thoughts, your unspoken sexual desires. It is time to become truly intimate with this ancient force and primordial lover of the moon goddess. He will keep you firmly rooted in your sexual orientations, for he embraces everyone who seeks him no matter their sexual preference and encourages you to explore the hidden and virile nature within your inner wild spaces.

LUSTY INCANTATION

Horny, for tonight's the night
Sacred union, sexual rite
Must man up and do the deed
Impregnate deep his virile seed.

RITUAL MAGICK

Make sexual union in a moonlit forest. Place one silver
candle and a gold candle on your altar and burn them down
simultaneously to balance your sexuality and the union
between moon and sun, feminine and masculine.

FAMILIAR'S MESSAGE

GOAT: I may be a stubborn old thing, but I'm not one to shy away from
a little head-butting. I have got all the guts, balls, horns, drive and power
to get you moving again; be it physically, emotionally or spiritually.
Take a good sniff: I am in the air all around you. Stamp on the ground:
I am under your feet. Look behind you: I am at your back. So potent
is my power that you must be very clear now of your intent. Use it for
a greater good and for an outcome that is beneficial, not detrimental
or vengeful. I do not judge, though many judge me, but abuse my gift
and you will be the one left to clear up the mess. If you are truly ready
to take things up a notch I am here. Just ask.

GOAT: POTENCY

Heavy-footed, stuck in a rut
Motivate to kick your butt
Potency of strength and force
Reclaimed, empowered, reinforced!

19   Monday

20   Tuesday
Third quarter moon.

21   Wednesday

22   Thursday

23   Friday
Kenneth Grant (1924–2011), ceremonial magician and an advocate of the Thelemic religion.

24   Saturday

25   Sunday

26 Monday

27 Tuesday

New moon · Nicholas II of Russia had a great fascination with occult magick and introduced it into the imperial court. He was connected with Rasputin, a mystic and seer who was murdered in December 1916. A year later the tsar abdicated his throne.

28 Wednesday

29 Thursday

30 Friday

Joan of Arc (1412–31), visionary and a patron saint of France; burned for heresy and practising witchcraft.

31 Saturday

1 Sunday

Fourth Witchcraft Act in England in 1735, instigated by parliament. The act abolished the hunting and execution of witches in the United Kingdom, as it was made a crime for any person to claim another person had magickal powers or was guilty of being a practising witch.

WITCHY TIP

Goat is a representation of the horned god, the masculine energy that drives the craft and as such the consort of the mother goddess. In this role goat is associated with nature, wilderness, sexuality, hunting and the life cycle and depicts the ultimate union of the divine and the animal – which includes humanity.

MOON MAGICK

The light of the bright moon shines upon you. The influence of the bright moon sheds light on what you are seeking, so draw now from its illumined power as you claim new strength from within. Having been cast down low for a while, allow the brightness of the moon to restore your vigour, might and energy so you can experience life at its highest magickal potential.

TRUTH INCANTATION

A path that glitters is revealed
Follow, for your fate is sealed
Seek, unlock the truth this night
And walk toward the shining light
Beltane magick is now said and done
So mote it be, with harm to none.

WITCHY TIP

Invite candles into your life to re-ignite the inner flame of passion, fuelling your ability to walk in your true light with full might and reclaim your magickal power. Light candles around the bath, in your bedroom and in ritual and sacred ceremony.

RITUAL MAGICK

Light a red candle. Write words on separate pieces of paper that represent potency to draw to yourself under the bright moon: strength, vigour, might, potential, power and so on. Burn each piece of paper in the candle flame in turn and say:

To empower my life bring me the same as
I set you alight in my lunar bright flame.

JUNE

Moon of horses, hawthorn, strawberry moon
Glorifying the full strength and light of the sun

June is busting out all over as the full bloom of roses and honeysuckle and warmer weather is celebrated. Named after the Roman goddess of marriage, Juno, sunny June sees the start of the wedding season and a June bride is considered to be lucky. June is also the halfway stage of the growing season for farmers, a traditional midpoint between planting and harvesting. The goddess is now the mother, and the sun god is at the height of his virility and life-giving power. Celebrations of fullness, expansiveness and achievements are awash with joy as the light reaches its peak and the longest day and shortest night of the wheel of the year are enjoyed.

LITHA: 21 June

GODDESS: Áine (Celtic/
Irish), faery queen of summer,
growth, love, luck, magick.

MOTHER: in her full
power, strength.

LITHA

Empowerment, celebration of light and full strength of the sun

This is the month that celebrates the sun festival known as Litha, or the summer solstice, when the sun is at its highest point in the sky and at its strongest. It is a time of intensification, of focus, development and determination as we connect with the sun to become stronger and claim our full self-power in celebration, honour and ritual. Those who are not aware of such a connotation may still, albeit unwittingly, worship the sun in other ways, for they partake in outdoor parties and barbecues and top up their tans during hot and sunny days. Celtic tradition honoured through tales and legends tells of a great battle that plays out at this time of year between the mighty holly king and the majestic oak king. At summer solstice the holly king wins supreme and stands proud through to winter, until at Yule he is cut down in his prime when the oak king wins and presides over the coming months until their next battle at Litha.

This is a time of year when you can tap into midsummer magick, as the veil between the worlds is thin: think Titania, Oberon, faery spells and faery rings of mushrooms, toadstools and flowers where those with an open heart are invited in to connect with the natural magick of the fae.

2 Monday

3 Tuesday
First quarter moon.

4 Wednesday
Since 2021 witch-hunts have made a resurgence in the Democratic Republic of Congo. Eight women were burned to death or lynched in September 2021, and between June and September there were 324 accusations recorded of people practising witchcraft.

5 Thursday

6 Friday
Alex Sanders (1926–88), occultist, high priest and founder of Alexandrian Wicca.

7 Saturday
Swein Macdonald (1931–2003), highland seer, mystic and occultist.

8 Sunday

9   Monday

10   Tuesday

The hanging of witches begins at Gallows Hill, Salem, Massachusetts. Bridget Bishop was the first witch to hang, in 1692.

11   Wednesday

Full moon.

12   Thursday

13   Friday

Gerald Gardner (1884–1964), high priest and founder of Gardnerian Wicca.

14   Saturday

15   Sunday

Muree bin Ali bin Issa al-Asiri (no birth records) beheaded in Saudi Arabia in 2012 for practising witchcraft.

MIDSUMMER INVOCATION

As I enter within this magical ring
My heart is open and ready to sing
Songs of the wood, words of the fae
Who guide me in, and show me the way
I call on the magic of Midsummer Eve
Whose mystic and mystery together doth weave
May power bestow me this very night
As I share my found gifts, for 'tis only right
With arms outstretched to the magical ones
I give honour and thanks. So now it is done.

MOON MAGICK

On 11 June your manifestation abilities will be at their optimum as the full moon shines upon you and her bright energy magnifies all that you place your focus and vision into. It is time to harness the power that magnifies from within, for the potency of your magick shines strongly during this moon phase and with the power of the summer solstice looming. As you witness the fading traits of the maiden, allow the mother aspect of the triple goddess, who is birthed at the full moon, to rise up within, for it is she who bestows abundance upon the earth and places the power of manifestation upon all witches. It is a potent time to work spells, for magick abounds. Allow the full moon to magnify and charge you up with its natural psychic powers. Remember that emotions run high at this time, making everything extra intense, so use this double whammy of intensity wisely and be completely clear about what you wish for as you weave your magick.

FULL MOON INCANTATION

Magnified magick of solstice and moon
I ask that my dreams will come about soon
As I harness the power of bright shining light
May power be bestowed on me this very night.

WITCHY TIP

Your psychic awareness is becoming highly supercharged, so harness it wisely. Keep expectations positive with magickal anticipation for maximum results, moon bathe for potent energetic nourishment and charge up your crystals under the full moon for optimum power.

RITUAL MAGICK

Place crystals in the moonlight to charge, and water scry under the full moon's light for clarity. Use sex magick, a powerful harnessing of intention coupled with the intensity of an orgasm and full moon energy. Make full moon water by placing a chalice of water under the moonlight to charge up for spells and healing. Add crystals for ultimate empowerment.

16 Monday

17 Tuesday

18 Wednesday

Third quarter moon.

19 Thursday

20 Friday

In 1597 King James VI of Scotland published a compendium on witchcraft called Daemonologie that arose from a royal obsession with witches. It was intended to convince sceptics that witchcraft was real, causing witch panics throughout Europe.

21 Saturday

Lilith, summer solstice, midsummer.

22 Sunday

23 Monday

24 Tuesday

25 Wednesday
New moon.

26 Thursday

27 Friday
Scott Cunningham (1956-93), author on Wicca and herbalism.

28 Saturday

29 Sunday
In India women are still labelled as 'witches' in order to take their lands, settle scores or punish them for not accepting sexual advances. It is estimated that between 50 and 100 women are killed each year for being practising witches.

Midsummer's eve magick

Faeries are known for their partying, particularly on Midsummer Eve. For those lucky enough to come upon some faery revellers they will speak of feasting, merriment and dancing around in circles. The reason why faeries dance this way is to build the energy of joy they exude into a cone of power and, hey presto, a tremendous amount of magickal faery energy is birthed into the world.

―――――――――――◯―――――――――――

Kitchen witchery

ROSE: a deep desire to be swept off your feet makes your heart beat furiously at the mere notion of romance. Romantic gestures such as love hearts, chivalry, pledges and chocolates can make you giddy with dreams of living happily ever after. Become in love with love itself, and the romance you yearn for will be ready to blossom as you honour your true feelings and appreciate the beauty that's all around you. As you breathe in deeply my sweet aroma, feel your heart centre swirl with sensual pleasure as it makes room for love in your life. I'll magnetise your aura to draw in all you seek on your quest for romance as you work with my petals and buds to cast spells of amour and create love potions. Place a bouquet of my red and pink variety in your bedroom to incite intimacy and delight as the heady heights of romance court you.

ROSE: ROMANCE

Red is for love, pink for romance
Petals swirl and join in the dance
To bring about romance, kisses and laughter
And be of your heart happily ever after
Rose magick is worked, with harm to none
So mote it be; there, it is done.

WITCHY TIP

Rose opens up your heart chakra. Deep within there is your inner temple where the goddess, who is *you*, truly resides. When your heart is closed you cannot access her.

Rose helps to open your heart, to commune with the goddess, for everything really happens within and then you see it without. As above, so below: so mote it be.

LOVE SPELL

Heartbreak, loss and rejection can cause your heart to shrink and make you defensive and guarded. Allow a love spell to unbreak your heart so you can become whole again. Hold a piece of rose quartz, light a pink candle, face the direction of south under a full moon and say:

Flowers of pink, crystals of rose
Bring me new romance so I will not close
My beautiful heart, for I'm longing to share
Compassion and kindness, to be gentle and fair
Desires recognised, I wish to ignite
My passionate dreams so that I might
Attract beauty and love into my world
May deep the love mystery now be unfurled
To bring about romance, kisses and laughter
And be of my heart happily ever after.

Blow out the candle and direct the smoke of the extinguished flame over your heart centre. Wear a rose quartz crystal close to your chest in your bra or as a necklace to invite love and romance into your life.

JULY

Hay, thunder, mead, oak moon

*The power of summer burns brightly, intensifying
passion and destiny*

The month of July signifies the height of summer in all its glorious radiance, as the sun beats down upon the optimum abundance of nature's full bloom. Now is the time to enjoy the gifts of the mother goddess, for your work is done.

The magick of summer invites intense energies of lust, passion, attraction, illumination, love, sex, sun and heat, so put down your tools, have fun and enjoy the carefree days of summer. Taking a well-deserved break to rejuvenate and have some fun is essential for your well-being on all levels, but be careful not to get burned as you enjoy outdoor parties, barbecues and sunbathing during this hot, passionate month and as you worship the sun and harness the power of the element of fire.

In magickal terms, the intensity of high noon is a perfect time to cast spells as you face the direction of south. As the heat of the sun breathes renewed passion into your workings and relationships you attract the energy of abundance, awakening your spiritual kundalini energy through lust, attraction and desire as you draw down the sun's energy. As the sun greets you it highlights the path you are to take toward your destiny so you can complete your life's mission.

GODDESS: **Étain (Celtic/Irish)**, the shining one, sun/moon goddess, lights the way on the path of transformation, toward balance, wholeness and rebirth.

MOTHER: Uncovering the light and strength within, beauty, sun, love, vitality of life.

30 Monday

1 Tuesday

Witchcraft Act in England repealed in 1951 and replaced with the Fraudulent Mediums Act.

2 Wednesday

First quarter moon.

3 Thursday

4 Friday

5 Saturday

Lucy Cavendish (1961–), best-selling author, witch and druid.

6 Sunday

7   Monday

8   Tuesday

9   Wednesday

10 Thursday

Full moon.

11 Friday

12 Saturday

13 Sunday

Margaret Murray (1863–1963), Egyptologist, archaeologist, occultist and folklorist; the first woman to be appointed as a lecturer in a university, in 1898. John Dee (1527–1608), court astronomer to Elizabeth I of England, occultist, alchemist and mystic.

SUMMER INCANTATION

Ignite the passion of summer and know
You are the power, the sacred glow
Love and passion stirred and invoked
Abundance is yours now the fire is stoked
Lounging, bronzing in the sun
Sea salt air and having fun
Food delights, cocktails too
Take this well-earned break for you
To be restored; take the charge
Enjoy the rest now. Bon voyage!

WITCH'S WISDOM

Sunny climates and beach parties fire up desires for a perfect bronzed beach body, so you boost your exercise, self-tanning and beauty regimes so you can look your best. In reality, though, what if this time of year makes you want to truly melt? Looks can be deceiving and a lack of confidence disempowering. Illusion uncovers every part of you that has ever been denied, repressed and disowned, and you may wish for the forthcoming darker months to arrive sooner.

Bikinis, shorts and swimwear might be on trend during this sizzling month, but as a natural witch you may prefer to dress day to day in the blackest black. It could make you feel protected and brave and is a wonderful disguise for insecurity. Witchy tradition directs you toward pointy hats, cloaks, long black dresses and buckled boots. Albeit yesteryear's fashion, it still holds power in its cloth. How freeing it is to dress in whatever clothing expresses who you truly are, wish to be or believe you are. Dressing up is a powerful form of boosting your inner power, for what you wear you attract and if the clothing you choose makes you feel empowered then so, too, will it boost your magickal work.

WITCHY ACCESSORIES

Don't forget to enchant your jewellery and wear magick rings, anklets, pendants and earrings whenever you need a boost of energy. Whatever you choose to wear should be a daily conscious ritual, for it is a powerful form of magick and especially when you dress up as the radiant, empowering witch you were born to be. It is time to dress up in alignment with your highest priestess or priest potential to become fully empowered.

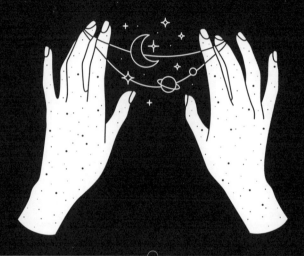

CLOTHING INCANTATION

Black pointy hat, long darkened cloak
Fantasy fashion for magickal folk
Dress up each spell with powerful intent
Empowering style with charmed jewellery and scent
Dress up in magick with harm to none
So mote it be: there, it is done.

14   Monday

15   Tuesday

16   Wednesday

17   Thursday

Chelmsford Assizes, a periodic court for serious crime and witch trials in Essex, England. Elizabeth Francis (1529–79) convicted three times for bewitchment and practising witchcraft; she was executed after the third trial.

18   Friday

Third quarter moon.

19   Saturday

Second hangings of the Salem witches in the United States; five women were executed in 1692.

20   Sunday

21 Monday

22 Tuesday

Mother Agnes Waterhouse (1503-66), the first woman executed in England for practising witchcraft.

23 Wednesday

24 Thursday

New moon.

25 Friday

26 Saturday

27 Sunday

Pendle witch trials started in 1612 in the York Assizes, a periodic court for serious crime and witch trials.

WITCH'S WISDOM

Mysterious symbols embedded into spells and candles and for other magickal purposes is indeed the sign of powerful witchcraft. As all witches know the very act of magick begins with a purpose that is birthed through intention, so as a witch you must take full responsibility for your thoughts and words and be consciously aware at every moment. Witchcraft is not just an array of random symbols and incoherent mutterings: no! Instead, magickal symbols are fused with specific intention depending on the purpose, and are most vital when it comes to seeding and speeding up your magick.

WITCHY TIP

Sacred symbols woven into your clothing
are your secret magickal weapon.

WITCHERY

When it comes to wearable witchcraft, the magick of colour is vital. Each colour carries a unique vibration to assist in empowering effective magick:

WHITE: purity and transformation.

BLACK: repels negativity and is protecting and balancing.

BLUE: when performing water magick and working with the direction of west.

GREEN: bestows faery power and fortune; wear it to perform nature magick and fertility rites.

PURPLE: powers up intuition, psychic awareness and spirituality.

YELLOW: opens up powers of communication, creativity and solar magick.

ORANGE: vitality and to create opportunities and inspiration.

PINK: promotes romance, self-love and beauty.

GOLD: enhances confidence, wealth and self-power.

SILVER: connects with lunar magick and mystic visions.

BROWN: important for grounding, resilience and security.

28 Monday

Huntington Assizes, a periodic court for serious crime and witch trials; Mary Hicks,
a witch of Huntington, and her nine-year-old daughter were both hanged for practising
witchcraft in 1716.

29 Tuesday

Jennet Preston hanged in 1612 at York Racecourse. Sarah Good hanged with four other women
from the Salem witch trials in 1612.

30 Wednesday

31 Thursday

1 Friday

First quarter moon · Lughnasadh.

2 Saturday

3 Sunday

Sigil magick

Sigil magick is a form of chaos magick: powerful spells and fast working. A sigil is a personally created symbol encoded with magickal meaning, intention and purpose. The power comes from the act of designing the symbol while focusing on the intent of its purpose, thus transforming and encoding the meaning and its magickal potential into your subconsciousness. You can activate the sigil simply by staring at it. Get creating in your own unique way and remember that the power comes from the coding process through your intention. The power of creation truly lies in your hands.

Sigil incantation

Magickal symbols and glyphs represent
Powerful purpose, creative intent
Spells now effective to cast and entrance
Empowering all witches to rise and advance
Sigil magick is worked with harm to none
So mote it be; there, it is done.

Witchy tip

Create and draw sigils of protection, love, abundance, self-power and anything that you need. Add power symbols to baking, water bottles, house, spells and rituals: you'll soon see tangible changes and results.

FAMILIAR'S MESSAGE

WASP: July is my favourite month to visit you. Am I not invited to sip and sup with you in your backyard? Mmmmm, tasty! Swot me and I will deliver a real sting from my tail. Unlike my honeybee cousins I can do this more than once, so be warned. If you seek revenge for serious wrongdoings, for words most foul spread about you, for acts in your name or for a hurt so profound that now it is anger and rage that keep you going I can deliver. However, revenge takes many forms and perhaps what you really seek is to be vindicated, to have the truth told or to have your name cleared. Think hard on this, for perhaps the best way to be avenged is to rise above all the chaos, to forgive, to release the hurt and take pity. You have the all the power now; it is your anger and hurt that feed into the drama. Remove these from any situation and you will inject a far more transformative energy into the situation than any pain from my efforts can manage.

WASP: REVENGE

Revenge is sweet, never to fail
Vindictive actions, sting in tail
Avenge torment without concern
Scores to settle in return.

WITCHY TIP

To dream of being stung by a wasp signifies the need
to look more closely at what is going on around you.
Something you have sown is going to come back to bite
you. When wasp is around know that jealousy is afoot.

AUGUST

Corn, holly, grain moon

*Celebration and gratitude
of the grain harvest*

This heady month of sun and fun is greeted as a time of opportunity and good fortune, for these are the carefree days of summer when the dreams that were seeded at Imbolc come fully into fruition and are now ripe for the picking. The first hint of autumn is witnessed as the hottest part of summer makes its promise to wane, through its shortened days and the first grains ready to be harvested. It's time to reap the harvest of rewards and appreciate and bless everything that comes your way, as you make the most of the remaining light and warm weather before fall and give thanks for the abundant growth of the passing season.

LUGHNASADH: 1 August

GODDESS: **Tailtiu (Celtic/Irish),** goddess of August and of the earth, the harvest and first grains; the foster mother of the sun god Lugh.

MOTHER: maturity, gratitude for earthly, physical sustenance.

4   Monday

Malin Matsdotter (1613–76), originally from Sweden and of Finnish descent, was burned as a witch.

5   Tuesday

6   Wednesday

7   Thursday

8   Friday

9   Saturday

Full moon · Akua Denteh (no birth records) was beaten to death for practising witchcraft in Ghana in 2020.

10   Sunday

World Day against Witch Hunts was created after Akua Denteh was killed in Ghana.

11   Monday

12   Tuesday
Madame Helena Blavatsky (1831–91), Russian occultist, philosopher and co-founder of the
Theosophical Society.

13   Wednesday

14   Thursday

15   Friday

16   Saturday
Third quarter moon.

17   Sunday

LUGHNASADH

Gratitude for gifts of the earth

Lughnasadh, or Lammas, marks the very first harvest of the year and the gathering in of the grains. It is when the sun god Lugh is celebrated: he is cut down in his prime only to rise up again the following year. Our ancestors looked forward to this important and busy time of year, a time of plenty for feasting in celebration of the first harvest and for honouring the natural cycle of life, death and rebirth, represented as the spirit of John Barleycorn (also known as Jack in the Green and Robin Hood). His time will come again, but for now the seeds planted earlier in the year have grown into an abundant crop and are ready to be harvested and stored in the grain barns, to see out the cold and barren months to come.

――――――――――――◇――――――――――――

LUGHNASADH INVOCATION

Today the wheel of the year doth stop
At Lammas, time to reap the crops
That were sown earlier this year
Celebrate the harvest cheer
Of wheat, of cereal, of the grain
Store it safely, before the wane
John Barleycorn is now cut down
From his prime, but look around
For Lugh, the sun god, shines from high
Over the fields from the sky
From Mother Earth we are blessed
Toil now over; soon can rest
But from the sow what did you reap?
Is it good or do you weep?
From hard work what have you earned?
Of the lesson what is learned?
May the magick of this day
Bless you now in every way.

WITCH'S WISDOM

August is your personal invitation to gather with others., for this is a time to be free, dance wildly, sip mead and lie on the grass listening to Celtic folk music or rock to your favourite bands. If you've been withdrawn of late it is because of a longing for the spiritual and mental stimulation that can only be found in the company of other witches. Online interaction is no substitution for meeting up with others when it comes to finding those who are like-hearted and who share a deep connection and the same beliefs as you. Likewise, if you've found yourself pulling away from those who appear superficially shallow, who do not feel the magickal pull of the moon, sun, stars and planets as you do and don't appreciate the beauty of nature then you are in urgent need of some witchy company.

Although you may prefer to magickally work alone, the importance of attending a gathering and mixing with like-hearted others is a must. Being a witch isn't all spells and rituals, you know: it's a celebration, so let's get this summer party started! There are many moots and witchy festivals out there where you will find gatherings of your kind, and that will infect a new sense of magickal fun into your life and work.

18 Monday

Lancaster Assizes, a periodic court for serious crime and witch trials, held in 1612. Pendle and Samlesbury witches – nine women and one man – were found guilty of practising witchcraft.

19 Tuesday

Salem witch trials held in the United States from 19 to 20 August 1692; one woman and five men were hanged for practising witchcraft.

20 Wednesday

Pendle witches hanged in 1612 at Gallows Hill in Lancaster, United Kingdom.

21 Thursday

22 Friday

23 Saturday

New moon and rare black moon (the third new moon in a season with four new moons), a powerful time for spell casting with shadows and light · Dorothy Good (ca 1687/88) was just five years of age when she was imprisoned with her mother Sarah Good in Salem. She was released nine months later, medically insane due to the horrors she had endured. She lost her entire family to the Salem witch trials.

24 Sunday

25 Monday

The entrance to Edinburgh Castle has a witches' well that commemorates the site where more than 300 women were burned at the stake. One of them was Dame Euphame MacCalzean, who was accused among other things of using a spell to sink the ship of King James VI as it entered North Berwick.

26 Tuesday

27 Wednesday

28 Thursday

29 Friday

30 Saturday

31 Sunday

First quarter moon · Raymond Buckland (1934–2017), high priest and occultist.

MOON INCANTATION

Casting spells solo gets the job done
But time to meet others, to have witchy fun
Gathering calls to meet at the moot
For laughter, sharing and friendship to boot.

WITCHY TIP

A moot is a gathering of magickal folk that is often held in the form of a meeting or as a small festival of music, dancing, beer, wine and mead. It's where you get the chance to hang out with other witches, share food and knowledge of folklore and magick and above all to make new friends, which is most welcome whether you're a solitary person or not.

KITCHEN WISDOM

HEMP: thinking outside of the box or looking at the bigger picture is the only way forward, although looking at a situation from another's viewpoint will help you understand the approach and attitude of others. My good reputation is often disputed, even though I've been used for textiles and rope for thousands of years. Nowadays my flowers and seeds are used in health foods, organic body care and other nutraceuticals, and I'm loved by vegans for my natural protein benefits and essential fatty acids. It is time to keep an open mind when I appear for, although my THC levels will not affect you like my cousin cannabis, my family holds the secrets of the universe to consciousness expansion through the consumption of our sacred plant medicine teachers.

HEMP: PERSPECTIVE

Expand your mind and take it high
Plant medicine will help you fly
My products are so good for you
Not just for hippies, witches too!
This magic is worked, with harm to none
So mote it be; there, it is done.

WITCHY RECIPE

Try this hemp energy bar to balance your hormones and for healthy skin, hair and nails. Mix together 1 cup of hemp seeds, 2 cups of soft dates, 1 cup of walnuts, ½ cup of raw cacao powder and ½ teaspoon of sea salt. Add in your favourite spices or herbs. Blend in a food processor until it becomes amanageable dough. Spread the dough out on a baking tray and freeze for two hours. Cut and serve and keep refrigerated.

FRIENDSHIP SPELL

We all need friends, and a good witchy friend can be hard to come by. Instead of shutting people out of your life, try opening up a little more and embracing an authentic relationship with someone who gets you. Write down the attributes you wish for in a friend and pop it in a photo frame. Light an orange candle and face west as the moon waxes and say:

An orange candle doth attract
Visualise to be exact
A friend that's loyal and is true
For witchiness in all we do
My heart is open to embrace
Invitations to their place
Share a spell, a laugh, confide
A friend to keep, who is by my side.

Allow the candle to burn down in front of the photo frame. The friend you seek will soon be unveiled.

SEPTEMBER

Harvest, hazel, fruit, barley moon

A time for gathering, resting, reflecting and celebration

As the cycle of the natural world moves further toward completion of the wheel of the year we find ourselves on the cusp of transition, just before the year begins to wane into darkness. Following the celebration of the grain harvest at Lughnasadh, which is now fully in and stored, the abundance and ripeness of the fruits of the earth the harvest queen bestows upon us at this time of year is acknowledged. The goddess is found in her mother aspect in the fading summer twilight or in the harvest moon.

As the full life of summer comes to an end we become witness to ripe fruits, nuts, squashes and the flaming fall colours of red, orange and gold as nature turns in on herself, with the promise of the darker barren months of winter to come. This was a time of preparation, gathering and storing for our ancestors, as the final fruit and vegetable havests were brought in and stored to last through the winter months. Traditionally, workers were paid for the upcoming year, annual dues were collected and accounts were balanced. Nature's gifts are in abundance, and as the soft autumnal sun declines and autumnal mists descend, soft ripe fruit falls gently from the heavily laden trees that fill the glade. It is time to celebrate and draw from the earth's bounty.

MABON:
22 September

GODDESS: **Banbha (Celtic/Irish),** earth mother, protection, fruitfulness, keeper of mystery.

MOTHER: contemplation, self-sufficiency, balance.

SEPTEMBER

1 Monday
First laws on spells and witchcraft passed in the Code of Hammurabi from 1754 BCE in ancient Mesopotamia.

2 Tuesday

3 Wednesday

4 Thursday

5 Friday

6 Saturday

7 Sunday
Full moon, total lunar eclipse · Margaret Ine Quaine (no birth records) and John Cubbon (no birth records) were executed in Castletown, Isle of Man in 1617. There is a memory plaque on Smelt Monument.

8 **Monday**

9 **Tuesday**

10 **Wednesday**

Tiberius Claudius, Roman emperor from 41 to 54 CE, executed 45 men and 85 women for sorcery.

11 **Thursday**

Silver RavenWolf (1956–), author of many books on witchcraft and Wicca.

12 **Friday**

13 **Saturday**

14 **Sunday**

Third quarter moon · The transmission of magickal knowledge was passed to humans from the watchers from the Book of Watchers, 1 Enoch, which is estimated to date from about 300 to 200 BCE. In chapters 7 and 8 the watchers teach humans magickal medicines, incantations, how to work with roots and plants and the signs of the moon, astrology and divination.

MABON

When day and night is in balance and the fruit harvest is celebrated.

Mabon is a recent name that has been adopted by witches and pagans alike to celebrate the autumn equinox, when daylight and darkness are in balance with each other and night and day are of equal length and in perfect equilibrium: dark and light, masculine and feminine, inner and outer. The name 'Mabon' is associated with the Welsh god of mythology, and also with faery queen Mab, who rules over the Unseelie Court of autumn and winter.

At this time of balance and celebration we are reminded that we, too, are a part of nature. This is a time of going deep within, of resting after the labour of harvest and reflecting to count your blessings for the abundance that has been bestowed upon you throughout the year. You must look at where you have been and what has been done during the preceding months and give thanks, which in turn will truly fill both your inner and outer gifts. This is when you reap what you had sown earlier in the year and harvest all that's now been made manifest from your earlier dreams and aspirations. It's also a good time to let go of all that is no longer necessary and watch it fall away, just as the leaves do at this time of year.

As you acknowledge and embrace your shadow side, bring it into balance with the light you already exude. Draw from the power of the cornucopia of abundance, a symbol for the wealth of harvest at Mabon, and balance your masculine and feminine energies so you can be both giving and receptive at this time of year in gratitude and perfect equilibrium.

MABON INCANTATION

Autumn's upon us, here at last
A time to reflect upon the past
Of the year that seems to have flown
Dreams were planted, now have grown
Mabon gifts you dark and light
Of perfect balance, both day and night
And so you must look deep down within
To check your equilibrium
Look back on past hurts, lessons learned
And use them so you won't get burned
Important to shine out far and wide
And to honour your shadow side
For both together make you whole
The two as one complete your soul
Light two candles: one black, one white
Representing your joy and plight
Eliminate all you do not need
But keep what you have to succeed
The harvest's in, give great cheer
And thanks for an abundant year.

GODDESS MAGICK

The fall festival of the autumn equinox, Mabon, is celebrated in Irish warrior Mab's honour. Queen Mab insisted that any man wishing to be king must drink of her mead to acquaint the king with feminine mysteries, for menstrual blood is known as the wine of women's wisdom.

15   Monday

16   Tuesday

17   Wednesday

18   Thursday

19   Friday
Fulda witch trials held in Germany between 1603 and 1606. Merga Bien (1560-1603) burned alive.

20   Saturday

21   Sunday
New moon · Partial solar eclipse.

WITCH'S WISDOM

As the mother of all creation, Gaia naturally knows and understands what is best for each one of her children. As soon as she hears your wishes she makes plans to bring about your desires – if they are suitable for purpose, of course. Do not be fooled, however, for new beginnings often mean drastic endings and Gaia will shake up your world until you take that first brave step into the unknown and unfamiliar. If you are coming up against blocks and can't see the way toward your dreams and goals you must release the need for material things as you become more in tune with nature. Burn essential oils and incense, grow plants, create gardens and honour the moon phases as you become an intricate part of the cycle of life, death and rebirth. If you're always complaining gratitude will serve you well, for it's about time you acknowledged the goodness in your life. Being grateful invites in beneficial experiences and more of the good stuff, so if you favour materialism over the natural world it's about time you embraced the storehouse within to stay healthy and aligned.

GRATITUDE INCANTATION

Complain and moan, no gratitude
Won't serve me well; 'tis plainly rude
Harvest's in, time to assess
Aligned, in balance, for success.

WITCHY TIP

Find an area of natural beauty or wildness. Alone and wearing natural fibres and barefoot, walk upon the earth and feel her energy rise up through your soles and nourish your spirit.

If you are feeling particularly weary lie down on the grass, soil or moss and allow Gaia to soothe your frantic thoughts.

GAIA BALANCE SPELL

Sit with your back against a tree. Light a green candle for prosperity and abundance, pour milk onto the earth for sustenance and say:

Mother of earth, oh, goddess Gaia
May your deep healing soothe all desire
From out of chaos, you created alone
With love that poured from your very breastbone
To share of the essence of the divine
Existential life for all of mankind
Oh, to awaken the goddess within
To embrace my gifts of deep feminine
In your honour I sing and I dance
Entwined among nature, a gift to enhance
And now I see that the balance in me
Reflects your pure divinity
Within my heart new strength doth reside
And shines forth new life, ne'er to hide
As I grow stronger I am able to see
That it matters not that 'I' becomes 'we'
I focus on honour and kindness to all
And the goddess of earth ensures I am whole.

Let the candle safely burn down and pour any leftover milk onto the ground for Gaia to receive. Say:

I invoke you now, to connect as one
So mote it be, with harm to none.

22 Monday

Mabon, autumn equinox · Salem witch trials in the United States between 1692 and 1693; eight people hanged for practising witchcraft.

23 Tuesday

24 Wednesday

North Berwick witch trials in the United Kingdom between 1590 and 1592; more than 70 people were executed.

25 Thursday

26 Friday

Witch-hunts are still being inflicted on innocent women and men, from Sub-Saharan Africa, India, the Middle East, the Amazon and Papua New Guinea.

27 Saturday

28 Sunday

FAMILIAR'S MESSAGE

RED SQUIRREL: my message as caretaker of the forest urges you to make time for play, to be sociable like me but to do so with a sense of sedulous care and not as a gossiper or slanderer. Be aware of how you come across to others and be diligent in your work. Harness my magick to increase your perception and instincts. As your awareness awakens to a full level of consciousness, notice the beauty and natural gifts all around you. Together we will fill your storehouse with all you need as we prepare for your future.

RED SQUIRREL: CONSCIENTIOUSNESS

Be mindful now and pay attention
Diligence relieves the tension
Must prepare, be not mistaken
Obligation to awaken.

WITCHY TIP

Squirrels are known as messengers of the gods, and the Irish faery queen Mab had one perched on her shoulder.

CERRIDWEN

OCTOBER

Blood, vine, hunter's moon

Season of witche and the olde Celtic year dies

October is the month we witness the death of nature. As leaves continue to fall we enjoy the vibrant colours of the season, darker nights and an abundance of squash. Now that the harvest is in and was celebrated at Mabon it's a time to prepare fruit-jam preserves and tinctures for colds and flu, using ingredients collected earlier from the earth, trees and hedgerows such as rose hips, apples and berries. The crone, who reigns over the harsher months, is cold and callous and beckons you with a bony finger to witness the death of nature and all that will assist you in moving forward.

SAMHAIN: 31 October

GODDESS: Cerridwen (Celtic/Welsh), keeper of
the gates between the worlds, grail goddess.

CRONE: bringer of darkness, death, blood and bone, the underworld.

SAMHAIN

An honouring of the souls of the dead, when the veil between the worlds is at is thinnest.

Hallowe'en conjures up ghosts, pumpkin lanterns and children shouting 'Trick or treat!' as they hungrily hold out bags for candy. It is celebrated at the end of October in both the northern and southern hemispheres. Traditionally called Samhain, this is an old Celtic celebration of summer's end. Fires were lit on the night of 31 October in the northern hemisphere and villagers burned crops and animals to share with their gods and goddesses and give thanks for the bounty of the harvest. The Celts believed that the souls of the dead in the underworld were set free for that night, some of which were welcomed and others feared. Costumes and masks worn were for protection from these spirits. The veil between the worlds is at its thinnest now, so we are more able to see and connect with the world of fae and spirit.

Samhain is still considered to be a time of connection and reflection on those who have left this world for the other, and to look at where we have journeyed from and to during the wheel of the year. The goddess in her triple form has become the crone, and we are invited to draw on her wisdom from deep within as she cradles us during the dark months to come and enables us to release all that no longer serves us.

SEPTEMBER · OCTOBER

29 Monday
First quarter moon.

30 Tuesday
Bridget Cleary (1867–95), Ireland's last witch, was burned to death over a fire by her husband, father, aunt and four cousins, who were convinced she was a changeling. It was claimed that the faeries had taken her, but the truth was a combination of Bridget's illness and suspicion of women with a mind and means of their own.

1 Wednesday
It is estimated that more than 200,000 witches were burned or hangerd in Western Europe.

2 Thursday
Arthur Edward Waite (1857-1942), occultist, magician, alchemist and co-creator of the Rider-Waite Tarot deck.

3 Friday

4 Saturday

5 Sunday

6   Monday

7   Tuesday
Full moon.

8   Wednesday

9   Thursday
Flavia Kate Peters 1968–), high priestess, faery seer and occultist, United Kingdom.

10   Friday

11   Saturday

12   Sunday
Aleister Crowley (1875-1947), English occultist, high priest and ceremonial magician.

SAMHAIN INCANTATION

Cauldrons boiling, lanterns shining
Ghouls and ghosts, groans and whining
Parties sweep across the land
Children, adults, hand in hand
Time of fun but must remember
As fires burn bright and glow with embers
Our ancestors who walked before
We honour thee and ask for more
Wisdom, tools, to help us be
The wise amongst us, let us see
Through veil, while thin, this very night
Protection in place, no need for fright
We welcome you and all you bring
Go deep inside and look within
To shed the old, a shamanic death
Embraced and warmed within the earth
Inviting in life anew
The goddess calls for it to be you
Through the year from maiden to mother
The end is now, to feel the other
In her glory stands the crone
Don't be afraid to stand alone
This sacred path leads you to be free
Go forth in strength. So mote it be.

WITCHY TIP

When you are treading a dangerous path of no return, focusing on the darker side of life invites in danger. You may have the power, but do you have the required control? Protection is vital when practising mediumship, trance and black magick.

WITCH'S WISDOM

The goddess Hecate walks between the worlds, bridging the gap between the living and the dead. She encourages the ethereal whispers, fleeting dark shadows and ghostly presence in the dead of night that you have witnessed of late, for her wish is for you to believe in the afterlife. She invites you to journey with her to the underworld. If you feel drawn to or seem to have a natural ability to connect with the spirit world and those who have passed over into her realm, it is she who has bestowed upon you the gift of communing with spirit and she encourages you to honour those who walked before you. This goddess of witchcraft is queen over the spirits of the dead, and her powers extend up to the heavens and preside over the earth. Hecate exists between and betwixt life and death. If you are at a crossroads right now choose your path wisely, in a perfect balance of light and dark.

HECATE INCANTATION

Hecate, goddess and underworld queen
Crossroads reveal the seen and unseen
Embraced within darkness, bark at the moon
Invoking the spirits who wish to commune
Hecate magick is worked with harm to none
So mote it be; there, it is done.

OCTOBER

13 Monday

Third quarter moon · All Templars living in France in 1307 were arrested and condemned for heresy and practising witchcraft. This is one supposed origin of Friday the 13th being unlucky.

14 Tuesday

Patrica Crowther (1927–), early mother of modern Wicca and high priestess, United Kingdom.

15 Wednesday

16 Thursday

17 Friday

18 Saturday

19 Sunday

20   Monday
Selena Fox (1949–), Wiccan priestess and pagan elder.

21   Tuesday
New moon.

22   Wednesday
Witch trials were held in Torsåker, Sweden in 1674 and 1675; 71 people were beheaded and burned as witches.

23   Thursday
Julie Aspinall (1964–), high priestess of the Coven of Gaia and founder of pagan and witches' festivals, Coventry, United Kingdom.

24   Friday
More than 2,000 magickal books were burned by Emperor Augustus of Rome in 31 BCE.

25   Saturday

26   Sunday

WITCHERY

Invoke Hecate at a crossroads during a dark moon phase. Place a black cloth on the ground on which to lay bones, then put a black candle to the right of the bones and a white candle to the left. Set an offering of bread and red wine in front of the bones and light the candles.

As you gaze into the flames, focus on inviting in Hecate by reciting the incantation above.

Safely snuff out the candles and pour the wine onto the ground for Hecate to receive in the underworld.

FAMILIAR'S MESSAGE

CROW AND RAVEN: our macabre presence in itself declares that battle has commenced. The sound of the primordial cry of deep wounding is consumed within the darkest of your emotions, as you sink into the despairing depths of the unknown. From deep in the abyss we will lend you our spiritual sight to see beyond your limited vision. We bring a message from between the worlds, for it is the mystery and magick of the old ways that beckon you when we soar into view. We are known as harbingers of change and transformation and have been observing you for a while, and we have come to reveal both the strength of your light and the deep magick that can be summoned upon from the darkness within. As you learn to fly between the worlds hurts of the past are released, so let go and allow the mighty span of our jet-black wings help you to rise. Feel the power and feel the expansion as you claim sovereignty over all.

WITCH WOUNDS

As a witch you may be no stranger to finger pointing, persecution and accusations. Think again if you believe that witch-hunts are a thing of the past, for how often have you been slighted for your quirky ways? When you are different, when you have a power that another wishes for themselves, you can become a threat. It is time to clear the timelines of the past, for they are a burden holding you back from your true power.

Take steps to protect yourself from threatening harm that's intended for you through jealousy, fear and discrimination. When you make a stand as a witch of the craft, when you can't be swayed into reacting to incitement, the persecutions of yesteryear are healed. As those past accusations are released a magickal resonance surges through you, invoking a force within to stand strong, speak up in truth and be proud to call yourself a witch.

WITCH WOUNDS INCANTATION

Sticks and stones, ancestors bones
Accused, secluded, so alone
Fingers pointing, friend or foe?
Stand strong, be proud of all you know.

27 Monday

28 Tuesday

29 Wednesday
First quarter moon.

30 Thursday

31 Friday
Samhain, Hallowe'en, a time to honour the ancestors who have gone before us in the name of witchcraft and were persecuted, burned, hanged, stoned and drowned.

1   Saturday
More than 170 women were executed in Rome in 331 BCE for practising witchcraft.

2   Sunday

WITCHY TIP

Carriers of magick, mystery and death, crows and ravens are closely
associated with the visible and invisible, the seen and unseen.
They are a magickal bridge between the worlds and are used
by witches to be their eyes as they can fly and spy for them.

KITCHEN WITCHERY

CLOVES: whispers behind your back or a hushed silence when you enter
a room indicate you are the topic of conversation. Rumours are spreading
and the word on the street is out. Where there's no harm in having a good
old chin-wag with your witchy friends, bad-mouthing someone's private
business should be avoided. You're no stranger to juicy gossip yourself: he
said this and she said that. It's just tittle-tattle! My antibacterial properties
are powerful enough to wash any gossipmonger's mouth out. Be watchful
of who you share intimate details with and play your cards close to your
chest. It's vital to keep your reputation in high regard, so I will assist in
purifying and raising your vibration and protecting you from any smear
campaigns. Burn me to put a stop to any gossip that is affecting you right
now, or push me into a red candle to burn in order to prevent and protect
you from any slander.

CLOVES: GOSSIP

Idle chitchat, dish the dirt
Untrue rumours spread and hurt
Burn me in order to prevent
Gossip, slander, detriment
This magick is worked, with harm to none
So mote it be; there, it is done.

WITCH WOUND
EMPOWERMENT SPELL

To heal from the wounds of yesteryear, stand under
a full or dark moon and boldly declare:

I am a witch
I am of power, that I know
I have the power to lose and say 'No!'
I have the power to change things around
I have the power to choose what I've found
I have the power to speak out and be
I have the power to truly be me
I am a witch!

ANCESTRAL MAGICK

Ancestral magick draws energy from the power of the bloodlines of the ancestors and is an honouring of your deceased loved ones and all those who have gone before, shaping your life through their actions in some way. Your lineage is old and the ancestors aren't only recent, but also ancient. It's important to honour the ancestors to keep their memory and spirits alive by giving thanks to them. When you do so they will impart their wisdom to assist you with your journey and witchy work.

NOVEMBER

Snow, ivy, dark moon
Reassessment, embracing loss and acceptance

Happy New Year! After the death of the year that we witnessed at Samhain, 1 November is celebrated by witches as All Hallow's Day, the start of the new Celtic year and the beginning of winter. However, November is regarded as being an autumnal month that offers a mix of cold and bright, as burnt-orange leaves continue to fall in the chill. The weather can be confusing with its bright sunshine accompanying much colder days, and it brings with it the promise of hard frost and sometimes snow. These harsh, biting days are a good time to defend yourself and define your boundaries with others, and for using darker magick to ward off harm.

As you prepare to face the harshness of the winter yet to come you can rejoice in a month of festivities, thanksgiving, fireworks and remembrance. It's a time of rain and great storms and therefore a good time for weather witching.

GODDESS: **The Morrighan (Irish/Celtic),** battle goddess of death and war, bane magick, the darker arts.

CRONE: death and rebirth, sovereignty, inner strength.

3 Monday

Petronilla de Meath (1300–24) was burned at the stake in Kilkenny, Ireland. Hers was the first known case in Ireland and the United Kingdom of death by fire for heresy.

4 Tuesday

5 Wednesday

Full moon.

6 Thursday

Mother Shipton (1488–1561), prophetess, soothsayer and witch.

7 Friday

8 Saturday

9 Sunday

Ama Hemmah (1947–2010) burned to death in Ghana for confessing to being a witch.

10 Monday

11 Tuesday

The witch of Endor was the first witch written about in the Old Testament, 1 Samuel 28:3-25. She was a female sorcerer who was visited by Saul, the first king of Israel, as she owned a talisman that could summon the dead. She predicted Saul's downfall.

12 Wednesday

Third quarter moon.

13 Thursday

Bridget Ellen Connors (1798-1874), or Biddy Early, the wise woman of Clare; her reputation as a healer, white witch and herbalist spread throughout Ireland. She outlived four husbands and her funeral was attended by more than 25 priests.

14 Friday

15 Saturday

16 Sunday

MOON MAGICK:
DARK SIDE OF THE MOON

If a dark shadow has fallen over you and there is no light to guide you, you are confronting the unknown. It is an uncomfortable place to find yourself in when your visual senses vanish within the dark places that emerge. Fearing all that you can't see, it is in the darkness that nefarious deeds hide and leave you feeling vulnerable and exposed. Unable to spot the threats that may be lurking in the shadows, a fear of what is unseen has left you shunning your darker side. However, avoiding the darkness for fear of its existence and repercussions could leave you exposed to danger. Falling victim to unforeseen circumstances, accidents, bolts out of the blue, abrupt unpredicted outcomes and startling revelations are on the cards. A belief that the lighter side triumphs over the dark urges you to place the necessary protection around you as you move forward and whenever you take up any magickal workings at this dark time.

SHADOW
INCANTATION

Danger lurks in shadows black
Hidden side, no turning back
Beyond control, unforeseen
Blinded to where I should've been.

RITUAL MAGICK

Face north and light a black candle.
Place black tourmaline at your feet and say:

Facing the moon, I lift up my arms
Black candle and crystal now banish harm
Keep safe and defend my energy flow
As I raise my vibration, allow me to grow
Now out of danger, protection in place
Magickal work safe to embrace.

FAMILIAR'S MESSAGE

BLACK HOUND: across the moors and mists of time I have travelled to warn you of what may occur. Do not ignore this message, for if you do so it will be at your own peril! My heightened senses can sniff out from miles away any impending storms on the horizon that could cause instability in your life. Fear not, for I will protect and guard you through the dark night and keep you safe. You have felt this uneasiness for a while and you need to trust that your inner feelings are correct. Never doubt them, for to do so would have catastrophic effects. I will fiercely guard your territory and you will hear me howl in your defence, shielding you from predators that would do you harm. Betrayal surrounds you, cloaked in love and light. They are not what they say they are and would seek your downfall, for below the surface are harmful intentions. I walk beside you now as your guardian, loyal and faithful, to prevent any harm coming to you in the future.

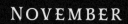

17 Monday

18 Tuesday

19 Wednesday

20 Thursday

New moon.

21 Friday

22 Saturday

Franz Hartmann (1838-1912), occultist, doctor, astrologer and theosophist.

23 Sunday

24 Monday

25 Tuesday

Helen Duncan (1897–1956), the last person imprisoned under the Witchcraft Act of 1735.

26 Wednesday

27 Thursday

Ireland's Salem occurred when witches were tried at the Islandmagee witch trials in March 1711, at the height of the Scottish witch-hunts. Eight women were found guilty of practising witchcraft and bewitching 18-year-old Mary Dunbar; the condemned women were alcoholics, disabled, smokers and visually unattractive and their deaths were not recorded.

28 Friday

First quarter moon.

29 Saturday

30 Sunday

Ralph Harvey (1928–2020), occultist, high priest and teacher.

KITCHEN WITCHERY

PATCHOULI: don't give up even though you may feel that your life has no meaning or direction, for I am here to change your outlook and remind you that having a purpose enables you to live life to the full. Seize the day and embrace the idea of achieving your goals to re-ignite your passion, and I shall give you good reason to get up in the morning. Use me in meditation as I transport your mind to far-off, magickal places with just one sniff of my musky and exotic scent. My potency will evoke nostalgic memories for your soul to awaken and remind you of why you are here on this beautiful planet at this time. Anoint your doors and windows with oil as a magickal defence or to repel negative influences, and use me in spells and rituals to attain the spiritual growth you've been seeking and mastery of the self.

PATCHOULI: PURPOSE

This sacred path is yours alone
Set personal goals for you to own
My potent oil will help achieve
Direction, purpose, to conceive
This magick is worked, with harm to none
So mote it be; there, it is done.

GODDESS GUIDANCE

If you feel a storm is brewing or you are being too defensive with others The Morrighan will help you face it. This isn't a time to avoid conflict or back down. She reminds you that with change comes chaos, which should be accepted and dealt with in order to move forward. Although she's a fierce goddess of battle, The Morrighan can assist you to take a softer approach if necessary while you build up your mental and physical strength. She will assist you to reign over the battlefield and claim your honour with the help of her gift of bane magick. This dark crone will protect you in all matters of battle, whether it's in defence, to take revenge or an internal conflict of the mind. Prophecy, magick and wisdom are the weapons she offers to lend you as you wield your axe furiously through your darkest moments. The Morrigan exists between and betwixt life and death. She dwells in the shadows and waits for you to claim your sovereignty as you walk with her between the worlds.

Light one black, one white and one red candle.
Let your imagination feed you images of all those
who have done you wrong or of fearful situations
or challenges you are fighting to overcome. Feeling
yourself consumed with dark emotions, stand under
the new dark moon on 20 November and say:

Attacks ensued to cause alarm
Enemies cause fatal harm
Boiling point; must seek revenge
Destroyed, this act must be avenged
Coercion forcing to conform
Enticement in its darkest form
Sticks and stones, cruel words of fear
Defend, stand strong, don't shed a tear
Death, destruction, loss and woe
Consume the mind; must let it go.

Let the candles safely burn down, then say with
your arms outstretched to the dark moon:

Let go of all that I hold dear
Won't let change instil new fear
Stand strong and watch the old decay
A new dawn welcomes me today
Withstand the storm to be free
Deliverance claims my sovereignty.

SOVEREIGNTY SPELL

DECEMBER

Wolf, elder, cold moon

A time of quiet introspection and expectation

Winter is a mystical artist that paints a breathless picture of landscapes adorned in jewels of sparkling frost and glistening ice. It is a time when your breath is visible on a cold, brisk day, when trees stand stark and bare and nature is stripped to the very core of its former glory. This is a season when mystery hangs in the air as dark nights draw in, enveloping the weakened, low-slung sun, and when the earth is steeped in deep magic and mystery that nurtures and restores all that reside within it. This is a time of looking deep within and withdrawing into your inner cave.

December is a month of hardship and discomfort that ensures trials and tribulations for those ancestors who faced the glacial callousness of winter, for she is a harsh taskmaster who takes no prisoners. It is a time for change, when you acknowledge and honour the cycle of death and rebirth. It's a time when hope is renewed and, like the trees of the season, you are stripped bare, naked and vulnerable as the macabre presence of the crone shrouds you.

YULE: 21 December

GODDESS: Cailleach (Celtic/ Scottish), the crone who rules over winter begins to fade as the returning sun shines new promises of hope, light and a fresh dawn.

CRONE: hideous queen of winter, bearer of storms, instigator of death.

DECEMBER

....

1   Monday

Malleus Maleficarum (Hammer of Witches), written in 1486 by Catholic clergymen, was
published in 1487 and endorsed the extermination of witches. The book had a strong influence
on the more than 110,000 witch trials in Europe that followed and was condemned three years
later. It was second in sales of books after the Bible.

....

2   Tuesday

Franz Bardon the magician (1909-58), occultist and teacher of Hermetics.

....

3   Wednesday

More than 123 people were persecuted in India for practising sorcery and witchcraft between
2016 and 2019.

....

4   Thursday

Full moon.

....

5   Friday

Pope Innocent VIII published a papal bull in 1484 that condemned witchcraft.

....

6   Saturday

Dion Fortune (1890-1946), occultist and ceremonial magician.

....

7   Sunday

8 Monday

9 Tuesday

10 Wednesday

11 Thursday

Third quarter moon.

12 Friday

Amina Bint Abdul Halim bin Salem Nasser (no birth records) beheaded in Saudi Arabia in 2011 for practising witchcraft.

13 Saturday

14 Sunday

YULE

A celebration of the rebirth of the sun, from the darkness growing into the light

Yule is the sabbat of the winter solstice, the shortest day and the least productive time in nature's annual cycle. This is the longest night, more than 12 hours of darkness as we wait for the dawn. The tradition of a mid-winter festival is ancient and was one our ancestors looked forward to through the cold barren days of December.

Yule is a celebration of the rebirth of the sun, for after the longest night the sun will again begin to grow stronger. It is a sacred time of solar rebirth when we bring into our homes the Yule log to represent the returning sun, mistletoe for fertility and holly for protection. This sabbat represents the rebirth of light. Here, on the longest night of the year, the goddess gives birth to the sun god and hope for new light is reborn.

This is a time-honoured tradition when our ancestors and faeries alike gathered to welcome the return of the sun. At the winter solstice the sun appears at its weakest, having waned in strength since peaking at the summer solstice, or Litha, six months earlier. Great cheers ring out in celebration, for on the very next winter's morn the sun will start its ascent as it heads towards the summer months once again. The birth of the sun; the light of the world; the new king is heralded!

This time the oak king prevails over the holly king to bring us the light half of the year. The holly king is the overseer of holly trees; he rules the forests and woods during autumn and winter after battling with the oak king at the summer solstice. They battle again at Yule when the oak king, the guardian of oak trees, wins and rules the forests and woods over spring and summer. Their battle reflects the balance of the seasons: the wheel has turned and we celebrate the re-emergence of light out of the darkness, bringing renewal of life and the promise of a successful future.

YULE INCANTATION

Faery folk tiptoe soft
Across the land of snow and frost
Toward a holly tree at Yule
'Tis time to cut it from its rule
For in this battle oak king wins
To lord o'er months to take through spring
And in the morn turn to the sun
Who is born again, the light has won
Each year the sacred wheel doth turn
Now Yuletide's here, 'tis our concern
To celebrate with joy and mirth
May bells ring out for peace on earth
So place the logs upon the fire
And make wishes of heart's desire
Honour the flames that warm the cool
With blessings to one and all this Yule.

WITCH'S WISDOM

Shrouded in mystery, the magnetism of the sacred sites found all over the world draws you in to connect with the power of the foundations upon which they stand. These ancient spots are situated on magickal meridians of potent earth energy that surge through each site and affect the physical, emotional and spiritual charge of those who stand upon the land. The earth's power connects deeply in with the ancestors and witchy seekers are drawn to gather at these powerful locations, such as the megalithic site of Stonehenge, at the winter solstice. Standing stones such as these hold the very wisdom of witches in their genetic coding, for the stones are wise teachers that have stood by silently while witnessing and absorbing every detail of spent centuries. They hold the key to your past. Strong foundations are a necessary basis for your witchy work, and they strengthen when you stand on ancient land. As the energy powers through you like a live current you become a conduit of full potential and soon become magickally supercharged as your personal power ignites.

15 Monday
Anna Franklin (1955–), high priestess and best-selling author of more than 20 books on witchcraft.

16 Tuesday
In Tanzania more than 40,000 people have been accused of practising witchcraft; many were tried and killed between 1960 and 2000.

17 Wednesday

18 Thursday
Edith Rose Woodford-Grimes (1887–1975), one of the first adherents of English Wicca and the working partner of author and Wiccan Gerald Gardner.

19 Friday
Ronald Hutton (1953–), historian specialising in witchcraft, paganism and British folklore.

20 Saturday
New moon.

21 Sunday
Yule, winter solstice, midwinter.

22 Monday

23 Tuesday

24 Wednesday

25 Thursday

26 Friday

27 Saturday

First quarter moon.

28 Sunday

SACRED SITE INCANTATION

Feeling the pull of old sacred land
Drawing you in to where ancient stones stand
Energy potent, feeling the flow
Magickally charged now and ready to go!

WITCHERY

Every sacred site has its own unique powerful and healing energy,
so whichever one you feel strongly drawn to will help charge
up your witchy magick. Even if you're unable to physically visit
a power spot you can draw on the energy of one that calls to
you through meditation, astral travel and in the dreamtime.

FAMILIAR'S MESSAGE

SEAL: survivor instincts have cut you off and recent events have left
you powerless and out in the cold. Your increasing sensitivity has
left you wounded and susceptible to emotional injury, and you could
well be seen as easy prey. Being wide open to criticism, verbal attack
and judgement has put you at the mercy of your doubts, fears and
uncertainties, which will dampen your resolve. Let me banish those from
your life who will not stand up to protect you. It's time to become thick
skinned, to be fully aware and not so gullible, yet you should try not to
act with such caution for defensive reactions could push the right people
away. Although there are opposing forces at play you don't necessarily
have to fight them all the time. Instead of drowning in self-pity, go with
the flow. Keeping aloof and unique separates you from those who would
bring you down and is vital for your survival.

SEAL INCANTATION

Isolation, frozen out
Susceptible to harm and doubt
At risk and bothered by the cold
Swim away now, strong and bold.

WITCHY TIP

Work with seal magick to drown your susceptibility to hurt by casting seal spells to make enemies vulnerable to attack.

GODDESS MAGICK

THE CAILLEACH: as the bringer of snow and frost, she is the OG of weather witches. She is the sharp, biting wind, the gatherer of black clouds and the bearer of storms, for she uses weather magick to influence the outcome of battle as well as to cause chaos. She harnesses the power of the four winds to storm rage across the land, and when gusts tear down branches and batter gathered crops this goddess of death is to be greatly feared. In the cycle of life nature must die before it can rise up and grow again in spring. Death is necessary in order to be reborn. The Cailleach is the bone woman, the blue hag of winter who promises that death is not the end.

WITCHY TIP

Long before the figure of Father Christmas was conceived, the far more ancient divine mother was associated with the winter solstice. The deer mother or Mother Reindeer carried the returning sun in her antlers and the sun was reborn.

HOOF AND HORN

Hoof and horn
All who die shall be reborn.

29 Monday

30 Tuesday

Maxine Sanders (1946–), high priestess and occultist.

31 Wednesday

1 Thursday

2 Friday

3 Saturday

4 Sunday

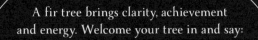

A fir tree brings clarity, achievement
and energy. Welcome your tree in and say:

A magick space I doth create
Tree is chosen, 'tis its fate
Welcome spirits, every one
Let's celebrate the return of sun.

In witchy traditions decorations represent the elements,
which are added to the tree over the 12 days of Christmas:

DAY 1, acorn garland: luck, prosperity and growth

DAY 2, shells: love and fertility

DAY 3, feathers: messages from spirit

DAY 4, cinnamon sticks: protection

DAY 5, quartz crystals: transformation

DAY 6, sprayed leaves: oneness

DAY 7, hazelnut clusters: inspiration

DAY 8, dried orange slices: good fortune

DAY 9, pine cones: enlightenment

DAY 10, holly with berries: protection and vigilance

DAY 11, mistletoe: rebirth and immortality

DAY 12, ivy: growth and renewal.

CHRISTMAS TREE CEREMONY

BANISHING CEREMONY

On the new, dark moon on 20 December place
a picture of the Cailleach on your altar.

Light a black candle and say:

*Bone goddess, I call upon you
To eliminate all in my life that's not true
Devour and destroy my guilt, fear and blame
Set them alight in the black candle's flame.*

Write on a piece of paper everything you'd like banished
from your life, safely extinguish the candle and say:

*By the protection of Cailleach, winter queen
I stand in my strength, now I am set free
From vows I have made through heart or in rhyme
Safe now in all directions of time.*

Place the piece of paper deep within your freezer.

WITCHY TIP

At the height of winter in Scotland it was customary for the head
of the household to carve the face of the Cailleach, as the Christmas
old wife, into a piece of oak to represent cold and death. It was
thrown onto the fire on Christmas Eve so that death would bypass
the house during the coming year. We know it now as the Yule
Log, although you are more likely to find a chocolate version
in most kitchens rather than a traditional log in the fireplace!

WITCHES OF ROYALTY

ANNE BOLEYN, *Queen of England*
Born: 1501 or 1507. Died: 19 May 1536
Briefly accused of using witchcraft against her husband
Henry VIII, which led to her death by beheading

JOAN OF NAVARRE, *Queen of England*
Born: 1368. Died: 10 June 1437
Accused of witchcraft

ELEANOR COBHAM, *Duchess of Gloucester*
Born: ca 1400. Died: 7 July 1452
Accused of practising witchcraft and died in prison

JACQUETTA WOODVILLE, *Duchess of Bedford*
Born: ca 1416. Died: 30 May 1472
Accused of practising witchcraft

ELIZABETH WOODVILLE, *Queen of England*
Born: 3 February 1437. Died: 8 June 1492
Accused of practising witchcraft

JANET DOUGLAS, *Lady Glamis*
Born: ca 1498. Died 17 July 1537
Accused of practising witchcraft and burned at the stake

CATHERINE DE MEDICI, *Queen of France*
Born: 13 April 1519. Died 5 January 1589
Accused of practising witchcraft

ISABELLA OF ANGOULÊME, *queen consort to King John*
Born: ca 1186. Died: 4 June 1246
Accused of practising witchcraft

GUNNHILD, *Viking queen*
Born: ca 910. Died: 980
Thrown alive into a bag and drowned
for practising witchcraft

WITCHES' MUSEUMS, MEMORIALS AND PLACES TO VISIT

Arnemetia's Magical Emporium, Buxton, UK

Mother Shipton's Cave, Knaresborough, UK

Museum of Witchcraft and Magic, Boscastle, Cornwall, UK

Pendle Heritage Centre, Barrowford, Lancaster, UK

Folklore and Witchcraft Museum, Falmouth, UK

Museum of Witchcraft and Wizardry, Stratford-upon-Avon, UK

Museum of Magic, Fortune-Telling & Witchcraft, Edinburgh, Scotland

Salem Witch Museum and Memorial, Salem, Massachusetts, USA

Buckland Museum of Witchcraft and Magic, Cleveland, Ohio, USA

New Orleans Historic Voodoo Museum, New Orleans, Louisiana, USA

Museum of Icelandic Sorcery and Witchcraft, Hólmavík Iceland

Witches Weigh House, Oudewater, Netherlands

Magicum – Berlin Magic Museum, Berlin, Germany

Hexenmuseum Schweiz, Gränichen, Switzerland

Witches Museum, Zugarramurdi, Spain

Museum of Witchcraft, São Publo Brazil

WITCH ORGANISATIONS

Children of Artemis

witchcraft.org

UK Pagan Federation

paganfed.org

Witchy facts

In Greenland in 1407 a man called Kolgrim was charged with practising sorcery and witchcraft for seducing a wife away from her husband. The husband claimed that Kolgrim used the ancient Norwegian magic of a singing spell to charm her away. These love songs, known as 'maiden songs', were forbidden on pain of death. Kolgrim was burned at the stake and the woman died of grief.

'Suffer not a witch to live': this quote, which is in the King James version of the Bible, has now been found to be mistranslated. A new theory states that the Hebrew words actually refer to herbalists or poisoners and not spell casters. The mistake was responsible for the witch persecutions that killed thousands of innocent women and men.

To stop witches from reciting spells a witch's bridle was used as a torture device. Made from iron, it had spikes across the tongue and acted as a muzzle. As a method of humiliation the witch was attached to a chain and paraded around in public. The witch's bridle was also used for gossipers.

A witch cake was thought to have the power to uncover a person's illness or possession incited by witchcraft. It was made from urine from the affected person and mixed with ashes and rye flour and fed to a dog. If the dog – the familiar – exhibited the same signs as the possessed individual it was deemed that the illness had been inflicted by a witch.

Suspected witches travelled long distances to Oudewater in the Netherlands to purchase official certificates stating they were heavier than air according to the town's scales. These certificates stated they were unable to fly and were less likely to be considered witches, therefore ensuring that the test of a witch by drowning was not applied to said witch.